Thomas Harrison Montgomery

A History of the Insurance Company of North America of

Philadelphia

Thomas Harrison Montgomery

A History of the Insurance Company of North America of Philadelphia

ISBN/EAN: 9783337253707

Printed in Europe, USA, Canada, Australia, Japan

Cover: Foto ©Suzi / pixelio.de

More available books at **www.hansebooks.com**

FRONT VIEW OF THE OFFICE, ERECTED 1880.

A HISTORY

OF THE

INSURANCE COMPANY
OF NORTH AMERICA

OF PHILADELPHIA:

THE OLDEST FIRE AND MARINE INSURANCE COMPANY IN AMERICA.
Began Business as an Association in 1792.
Incorporated 1794.

PHILADELPHIA:
Press of Review Publishing and Printing Company.
1885

CONTENTS.

ILLUSTRATIONS.

Charles Platt

President

SEVENTH PRESIDENT, 1879.

PREFACE.

THIS history of the oldest joint-stock insurance company in the United States, now venerable in its age, and national in its standing, was undertaken on the request contained in the following letter of President Platt:

INSURANCE COMPANY OF NORTH AMERICA,
232 Walnut Street,
Philadelphia. April 19, 1881.

DEAR MR. MONTGOMERY:

Our Board at their last meeting passed the following resolution:

That the officers be requested to cause the history of this Company to be written, and you were mentioned in connection as the only person competent to perform the service satisfactorily.

May I ask you if you will undertake the work in your leisure time?

Yours truly,

CHAS: PLATT.

THOS. H. MONTGOMERY, ESQ.

The connection happily held by the compiler with the Company during the years 1879 and 1880, when in charge of an important section of its fire branch, afforded him favorable opportunities of conning its early and later records, and Mr. Platt, sharing in the interest the review of these naturally aroused, encouraged a more systematic search among its papers and files for all those facts and incidents which would best illustrate the origin and growth of the institution.

There is very much in its annals inducive to a study of those principles of underwriting, which in a century have testified to such development in this the youngest of nations. Accepting the practices and customs of our parent country, we yet have had to apply and interpret them as the exigencies of our growth under new conditions of trade and society have demanded, and both in marine and fire underwriting to adapt these traditions of our forefathers to present practice, as the material and mechanical development of the country required.

There is, as well, ample store for illustration of the financial growth of the country, as in more than nine decades it has passed through all the vicissitudes the people have endured in that time in the varying fluctuations of the commercial world; but it found its Policy of Insurance indemnifying it against the hazards of financial failure in its own good credit and hearty pluck, and in its faithful management by wise and discreet officers.

The scope of this compilation, however, will not permit the discussion and elaboration of those important features which a perusal of the company's records offers temptingly to view. And it may suffice for its friends and well-wishers to find in these pages those salient points of interest which testify to its inception, its growth, and its present maturity: to find how well its foundations were laid, how the superstructure has grown amid the sunshine and storms of almost a century; and to learn somewhat of the chief actors in its concerns, whose guiding hands have in these busy years, one by one, brought it to its present eminence and usefulness.

The records and files of the Company, which have been singularly well preserved, afford a large amount of material, which in its detail, would both instruct and entertain; but it is trusted that enough is here produced to portray with sufficient distinctness, what has been attempted amidst the claims of many duties, a History of the Insurance Company of North America.

T. H. M.

PHILADELPHIA, 1 June, 1885.

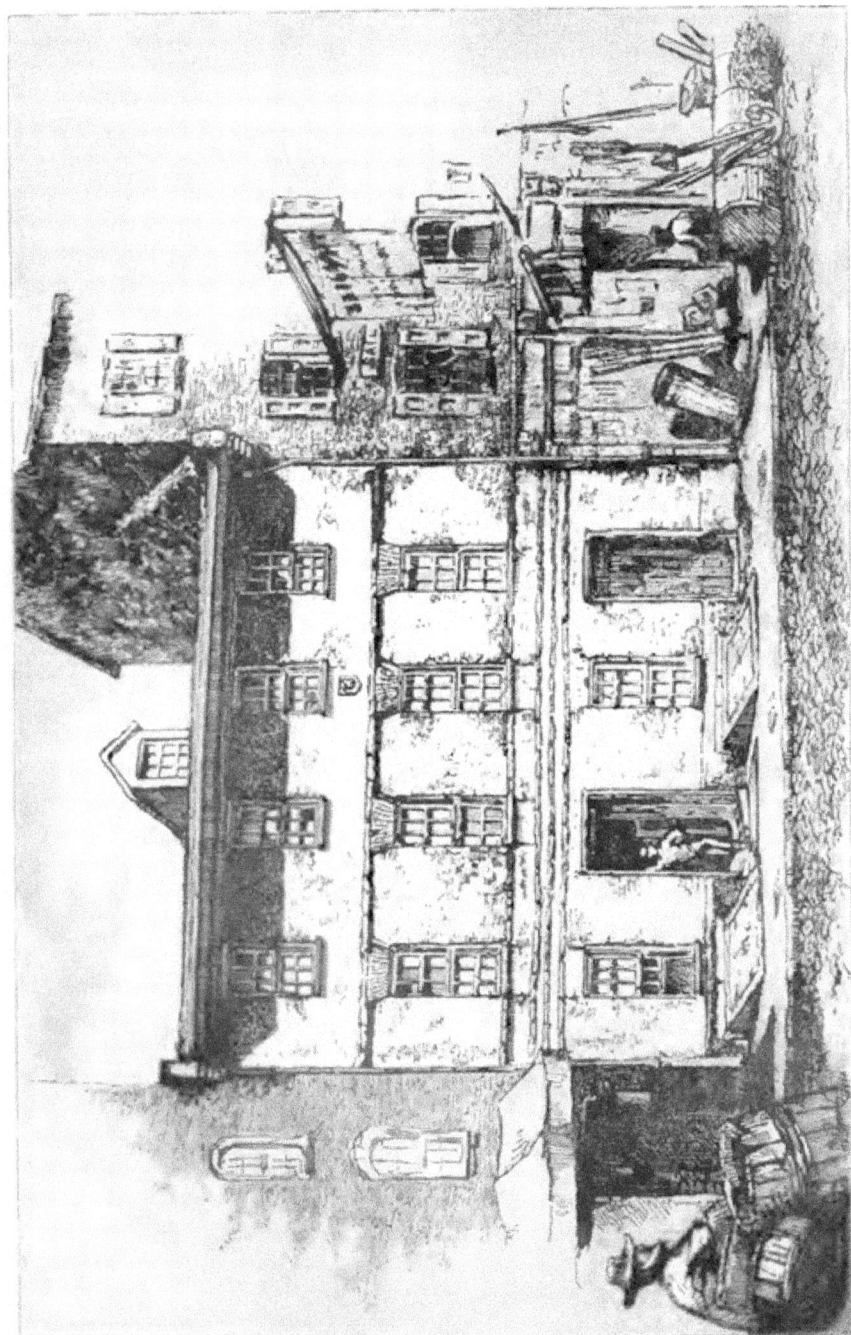

THE FIRST OFFICE OF THE INSURANCE COMPANY OF NORTH AMERICA, 1792-94

A HISTORY

INSURANCE COMPANY OF NORTH AMERICA.

I.

ORGANIZATION.

THE INSURANCE COMPANY OF NORTH AMERICA had its origin in THE UNIVERSAL TONTINE, which was projected in the city of Philadelphia early in the year 1792. Sundry citizens, to whom were added some of Boston, planned the scheme of a Tontine, a system which had many attractive and plausible features, "for the purpose of raising a fund upon lives, to be applied to the charitable and other uses." The subscription books were to be opened on the twentieth day of March, 1792. It was founded upon the plan of The Boston Tontine Association, a copy of whose Constitution, printed in 1791, was submitted to the present subscribers, and yet remains among the files of this Company. The Boston failed of its original objects, and eventually took the form of a State bank, The Union: a like project in New York came to naught about the same time. Among the promoters in

the Boston Association was Mr. Samuel Blodget, jr., a son-
in-law of the Rev. William Smith, D. D., the first Provost
of the College and Academy of Philadelphia. A friend and
correspondent of his in Philadelphia, Mr. Ebenezer Hazard,
was kept informed of its progress, and when it failed of
success, it was by the latter's intervention that Mr. Blodget
concluded upon attempting the Fund in this city; and it
was due to this instrumentality that some of the Boston
subscribers transferred their interests to the Philadelphia
scheme.

The subscriptions to The Universal Tontine, as it was
here called to avoid the appearance of only a local scope,
were opened on the day named. "In order to pursue the
preliminary steps for establishing the Society," there were
"appointed five agents, to wit: John Maxwell Nesbitt,
Walter Stewart, Jasper Moylan, Samuel Blodget, junior,
and John Dewhurst, Esquires, and one Secretary, to wit,
Ebenezer Hazard." In due time one hundred and eighty-
seven persons signed the Articles of Association, their
shares, however, numbering in the aggregate but eight
thousand four hundred, when the required limit was one
hundred thousand shares. At the close Mr. Blodget subscribed, in conformity to the third article of the Association, to fifty thousand shares to transmit for sale to Boston,
no agent or other subscriber being allowed more than fifty
thousand shares, "in order to prevent the shares from being
monopolized by the citizens of any one State or District, to
give effect to the beneficent design of the Institution."

But no one locality seemed desirous to monopolize this
beneficence. Pursuant to the Articles of Association, a

general meeting of the subscribers was held at the State
House on Saturday, 3 November, 1792, pursuant to a public
call, advertised in the papers from 15 September to the date
of meeting, "when the agents represented to them the state
of the subscriptions, and the improbability of success in
carrying the plan of the Tontine into effect; that a similar
attempt had failed at Boston, and another at New York;
that Tontines in general appeared to be in disrepute; that
no subscriptions to The Universal Tontine had been received for a considerable time; that many who had subscribed were dissatisfied, and were desirous that either the
Association should be dissolved or the Funds appropriated
to some other use; and that the idea of a general Insurance
Company had been suggested, and appeared to meet with
public approbation." Upon this a committee was unanimously directed to be formed "to devise, digest, and report
such other use, or uses, as they shall deem eligible and
most beneficial to the Society for employing the Fund
raised," and Messrs. Nesbitt, Moylan, Stewart, Blodget,
with Alexander James Dallas, Matthew McConnell, and
Edward Fox were appointed such committee. This direction to the fund may fairly be laid to the voice of Mr.
Nesbitt, who, in his extended experience as a policyholder,
and also as an underwriter himself, foresaw the great possi-
bilities of a large association engaging in the business of
underwriting the ventures of our citizens in the growing
commerce of the port; and to him we shall see was committed the first presidency of this wise effort.

To the adjourned meeting, held at the same place on 12
November, this committee reported "that in their opinion

it will be for the interest of the concerned to change The Universal Tontine into a general Insurance Company, and submitted a plan for that purpose to the consideration of the meeting," and this plan being read, it was unanimously resolved, " That The Universal Tontine Association be and it is hereby changed from its original objects and converted into a society to be called THE INSURANCE COMPANY OF NORTH AMERICA," and the Plan was referred for consideration in detail to an adjourned meeting, which was held at the same place on Monday, 19 November, when it was unanimously adopted.

The subscriptions to this came in good number, and by 1 December the minimum number of forty thousand shares were taken, when, agreeable to Article VII. of the Plan, the Secretary called a meeting for the 10th, at the same place, for the election of fifteen directors.   Mr. Hazard received these subscriptions at his new house, which he had recently built at No. 145 (now 415) Arch street, where also, probably, the Tontine subscriptions had been received by him.   At this meeting General Walter Stewart was appointed Chairman, and Messrs. Hazard, Francis Ingraham and Fox, Tellers, who reported the election of the following Directors:—

SAMUEL BLODGET, JR.,	JASPER MOYLAN,
JOSEPH BALL,	CHARLES PETTIT,
MAGNUS MILLER,	THOMAS L. MOORE,
MICHAEL PRAGER,	JOHN ROSS,
JOHN M. NESBITT,	WALTER STEWART,
MATTHEW MCCONNELL,	WILLIAM CRAMOND,

The following notification was pub:
:lished in Fenno's, Bache, Dunlap's & Claypoole's Papers;
viz.:
        Agreeably to the Seventh Article of
their Constitution Notice is hereby given to the members
of the Insurance Company of North America, that
Forty Thousand Share are subscribed; and that a
general Meeting of the Subscribers is to be held
at the State House in this City, on Monday, the
10th Ins.t at 10 O'clock, A.M. when the Directors are
to be chosen. —
                     Eben Hazard Sec'y

    The Holders of Certificates in
the late Tontine Association who
intend to become members of the
Insurance Company, are desired
to call at N.o 145, Arch Street where
their Subscriptions will be received.
    Phil.a Dec.r 1.st 1792. —

                          Dec.r 10th 1792.
    The Insurance Company met, pursuant to the
above Notice.
    General Walter Stewart was appointed Chairman,
& the Meeting proceeded to the Choice of Directors. —
    Mess.rs Hazard, Ingraham, & Foy, were appointed a
Committee to receive & count the Votes; which, upon Exami:
:nation stood as follows, viz:

For Samuel Blodget Jun.r	4136.	John Ross	3970
Joseph Ball	4120.	Walter Stewart	3920
Magnus Miller	4090.	William Cramond	3916
Michael Prager	4090.	John Leamy	3590
John M. Nesbit	4050.	John Sodwick	2496
Matthew M.Connell	4050.	John Barclay	2420
Jasper Moylan	4040.	Robert Ralston	2348,
Charles Pettit	4038.		
Thomas L. Moore	4016		

If some few Votes were given for other Candidates: —
upon the whole it appeared that the Fifteen Gentle:
:men first above mentioned were elected Directors, to
continue in Office until the second Tuesday of January
next.
                             At

JOHN LEAMY. JOHN BARCLAY,
JOHN SWANWICK,

who are named in this order according to the number of their votes respectively.

Thus was formed and brought into existence THE INSURANCE COMPANY OF NORTH AMERICA, in the same room where was transacted, sixteen years before, that memorable scene which forever names it INDEPENDENCE HALL; and the Directors at once took steps to form their plans under the eighth of their Articles of Association, "To make such Insurances upon Vessels and Merchandize at Sea, or going to Sea, or upon the life or lives of any person or persons, or upon any goods, wares, merchandize, or other property gone or going by land or water; and at such Rates of Insurance or Premium as they shall deem advisable."

II.

EARLY MARINE UNDERWRITING IN PHILADELPHIA.

THIS first attempt to establish a corporate association for effecting marine assurances in Philadelphia merits some notice of the conduct of that business in the earlier years of the city's history. Resort was had by the early shippers to the private underwriters of Great Britain, and early mention of London underwriting for American interests is found in the *Penn and Logan Correspondence*, though William Penn's scruples as to insuring his property often prevailed. James Logan writes him in 1701: "Notwithstanding thy tenderness about insurance, I hope there is some made."—i. 80. But Penn's tenderness seemed to prevail only when a promising risk was despatched. He writes Logan, 6 September, 1702: "I shall be glad if this dull sailer [Cantico] gets as safely as the Hopewell. I am tender as to insurance, and did nothing in it for the Hopewell."—i. 133. He seems to have been tender, also, as to the credit of the underwriters, doubtless deeming but little dependence would be placed upon a business which might not have the sanction of Heaven. He writes 16 February, 1705, to Logan: "J. Askew ensured £100 upon thy letter, but the ensurer broke, and the twenty guineas lost. This done upon the former intimations. Ensurers fail much."—i. 353.

In 1721 Mr. John Copson opens an office or agency for the procuring of home insurances from local capitalists, and in the *American Weekly Mercury* of 25 May, 1721, he advertises his plan as follows : —

"ASSURANCES *from Losses happening at Sea, &c., being found to be very much for the Ease and Benefit of the Merchants and Traders in general; and whereas the Merchants of this City of* Philadelphia *and other Parts have been obliged to send to* London *for such Assurance, which has not only been tedious and troublesome, but even very precarious. For remedying of which,* An Office of Publick Insurance on Vessels, Goods and Merchandizes, *will, on* Monday next, *be Opened, and Books kept by* John Copson *of this city, at his House in the* High Street, *where all Persons willing to be Insured may apply: And Care shall be taken by the said* J. Copson *That the Assurers or Under Writers be Persons of undoubted Worth and Reputation, and of considerable Interest in this City and Province.*"

It was within a few years of this announcement that there was published, in 1725, in Philadelphia, by S. Keimer, the first book in America in which reference is made to insurance; it was printed by Benjamin Franklin, and its interest increases from the fact it was the first book printed by him.   It was Franklin who was, in 1752, greatly instrumental in establishing the first insurance company on the continent, The Philadelphia Contributionship for the Insurance of Houses from Loss by Fire.   The author of this early work was Francis Rawle, the founder in America of the family of that name, and was entitled *Ways and Means for the Inhabitants of Delaware to become Rich*, and in it he classes insurance as a branch of trade, which, while helpful to the adventurer on risks by sea, would as well be promotive of commerce and agriculture.   But Mr. Rawle's paragraph so well expresses the benefits of insurance that he is entitled to the insertion here of his own argument, which cannot be improved on in the language of to-day, in showing that insurance is, in truth, the foundation of all solid business enterprise :—

> " Having thus far difcours'd of moft of the Branches of Trade we are capable of, there is yet one great Encouragement, to adventure in the Difcovery and Profecution of new Markets ; more fafe to the induftrious Adventurer ; namely an *Infurance-Office* in one or more of thefe Colonies ; which is the interefting of divers in the Lofs or Profit of a Voyage, and is now become so much the Practice of *England*, that Infurance may be had in divers Cafes as well againft the Hazards at Land, as Cafualties at Sea, which muft be acknowledged not only to be fafe, but a great Encouragement to adventure ; for it may fo happen that a Perfon may fometime adventure his ALL, and then in case of a Lofs he may be rendered uncapable of a future Trade, to the Difadvantage of the publick, and (it may be) to the Ruin of himfelf ; whereas could he get a part of his Intereft either of Ship or Cargo infured, (tho' in Cafe of fafe Arrival he parts with a part of his Profit, yet) in Cafe of lofs, he is fecur'd of fuch part as he infureth, which may be fufficient Bottom to begin a new Adventure : How far this may conduce to the Trade of this River, is obvious to any Man of Thought. Now whereas there has been fome Attempts made at *Philadelphia*, which dropt and prov'd abortive, (for what Reasons we never could learn) we humbly propofe to the Legiflature that an Office be erected and supported by a Fund arifing out of the Intereft of the Loan-Office. This will be a good and fafe Bottom, and cannot be eafily overfet by a few loffes ; and we conceive will contribute to keep up the Value of our Paper-Credit by promoting of Trade, Navigation and Building of Ships, and in Confequence, of great Advantage to this River : Which we refer to the Confideration of the Merchant."
> —pp. 62-63.

From the date of Mr. Copson's opening an office in 1721, of the operations of which we are without any particulars, and which may have been included by Mr. Rawle among those "attempts made at Philadelphia, which dropt and prov'd abortive :" many years elapse before we have record of another Insurance Office. We find, however, from the

No. 201   Assurance, Company of North America

Whereas John Leamy

upon all Kinds of lawful Goods and Merchandize, laden or to be laden aboard the good *Brig* called the *Baron De Carondelet*

In Case of Loss, such Loss is to be paid in ten Days after Proof and Adjustment thereof. The Amount of the Note given for the Premium, if unpaid, being first deducted.

This Insurance is declared to be made on Cash.

It is mutually agreed that if the above Cash shall not be shipped on board the Baron De Carondelet, but on board the Brig Ceres, Andrew Armstrong, master, the above Insurance shall be considered as made on the said Brig Ceres, and be equally binding on the Parties as if the Brig Ceres, and not the Baron De Carondelet, had been named in this Policy.

The Assured, warrants the above Cash to be American Property.

2000   Two thousand Dollars for the Assurance   Ino. of the Assurance

EARLY MARINE POLICY OF THE INSURANCE COMPANY OF NORTH AMERICA, 1793.

MS. journal of the Hon. John Smith, the originator in 1752 of the Philadelphia Contributionship, that local underwriting was resorted to by the merchants in his day. On 13 June, 1746, he writes he "was busy with the insurers of the sloop, but could not get them to settle till they see whether they shall have her or not." And on 1 December, 1749, "William Callender and I were at the Insurance office in the morning about business"; and we see that he himself begins to underwrite, for on 10 November, 1750, he records he "was at the Insurance office, and began to underwrite." This was the insurance office of Mr. Joseph Saunders, which at this time was located on Reese Meredith's or Carpenter's Wharf. This is, in fact, the first one of whose operations we know anything, and which was the forerunner of others which became equally well known. Mr. Joseph Saunders was an eminent citizen and prominent member of the Society of Friends, who began issuing his policies, all prefaced by the invocation, "In the Name of GOD, Amen," at his store on Reese Meredith's Wharf, above Walnut street (*Pennsylvania Gazette*, 28 July, 1748). In 1752 we find he

> "IS remov'd from his late store on *Reese Meredith's* or *Carpenter's* Wharf to the Houfe wherein *Ifrael Pemberton*, the Elder, lately liv'd, in Water-Street, the next door to *James Pemberton's*, at the Corner going down to Cheftnut-Street Wharf, where he continues to fell," &c., &c.
>
> *Penn'a Journal*, 10 March, 1752.

Within a few months he advertises:

> "NOTICE is hereby given, That the INSURANCE OFFICE for Shiping and Houfes is kept by Jofeph Saunders at his Houfe, where Ifrael Pemberton, fen., lately lived, near the Queen's Head in Water-ftreet."
>
> *Penn'a Journal*, 25 June, 1752.

2

This was the first office of the Philadelphia Contributionship, Joseph Saunders being the first Clerk of that association, which had been organized the previous April, wherein he was succeeded in 1754 by Robert Owen. This is the first Fire Insurance advertisement published in Philadelphia.

In 1756 we find him

> " Remov'd to the corner of Chefnut and Water-ftreets, the next door but one to where he formerly liv'd."
>
> *Pennsylvania Gazette*, 10 October, 1754.

To a later advertisement he adds a postscript:

> " N. B.—The INSURANCE OFFICE for SHIPPING is Kept by him as ufual."
>
> *Pennsylvania Gazette*, 8 July, 1756.

He again moves four years later:

> " JOSEPH SAUNDERS is removed from his late Dwelling, near Chefnut-ftreet Wharff, higher up Chefnut-ftreet, between Front and Second-ftreets, and next Door, but one, to John Reily's,* where he continues to fell fundry Sorts of Goods, and Keeps an Infurance office for Shipping, as ufual, and hopes his Friends who have been pleafed to employ him in that Way will ftill continue their Favours."
>
> *Pennsylvania Gazette*, 23 October, 1760.

This office was on the south side of Chestnut,† about six

---

* This gentleman undertook to insure lottery tickets, as was done some years later by the clients of Kidd and Bradford. To an advertisement of St. Paul's Church Lottery there is added:—

> N. B. John Reily, of this City, Conveyancer, will infure Tickets in this Lottery at a very low Premium."
>
> *Pennsylvania Gazette*, 29 January, 1761.

† See the advertisement of M. Symonds in *Pennsylvania Chronicle*, 2 May, 1768, of a

> " Removal to the new shop in Chefnut street, the fixth door from Second Street, nearly opposite to Mr. Joseph Saunders, merchant."

or seven doors east of Second street, and we find him advertising here up to 1768.*

The next office we find is that of Thomas Wharton.

> "On Carpenter's wharf, where Joseph Saunders lately kept:"
> "N. B.—The Insurance Office is there as formerly."
>
> *Pennsylvania Gazette,* 7 May, 1752.

This announcement of Mr. Wharton's enterprise led to Mr. Saunders's advertisement of the following June, above quoted, by which he sought to remind his friends that he yet continued his insurances in his new quarters. He had not before this competition arose advertised his insurance

---

* This worthy citizen was born 8 January, 1712-13, at Farnham Heath, in the parish of Farnham Royal, County of Bucks, the third child of Joseph and Susannah Saunders, and brought a certificate from Friends' Meeting in London, 12 February, 1733, to Philadelphia Yearly Meeting. He married Hannah, daughter of John Reeve, of Philadelphia, 8 January, 1741, and died 26 January, 1792. Of his large family of children but seven married, and his descendants find representatives in many of the prominent families of Philadelphia at this day. His son John married Mary Pancoast, and of his daughters, Sarah married William Redwood, Susannah married William Hartshorne, Mary married Thomas Morris, Hannah married Mordecai Lewis, Rachel married Joseph Crookshank, and Lydia married Samuel Coates. The earliest policy from his office now known to exist was issued to John Kidd, and underwritten by John Mifflin, Archibald McCall, Samuel McCall, junior, and Augustus Hicks, in the amount of £450, on Goods from Philadelphia to London, at four per cent., bears date 25 April, 1749 (o.s.), and is endorsed by him, "Reg^d in Book B, fol. 83," by which we can approximate to the beginnings of his insurances. A policy of his, dated 27 May, 1761, conforms to the new style, and omits the "In the Name of GOD, Amen," which phrase had been omitted by Thomas Wharton in the policies issued by him. They still retain the phrases, however, "Whereof is Master, under GOD, for this present voyage," &c., &c. It was to Mr. Saunders's office that Colonel Thomas White refers in the following letter to his friend Mr. Thomas Harrison, of Baltimore County, written 24 April, 1755:—"On my coming to Town I went to ye assurance office and ordered ye Policies to be made out, but could get only ye 75£ on ye Brig Philip & James underwrit; they having already fully ventured on ye other vessel; the reason is, that very few will underwrite on a vessel from Maryland. Mr. Meredith has signed for ye above 75£ in Goods at 3½ p ct so yt I paid £2. 17. 6."

office : his assuming the Clerkship of the Contributionship at this time doubtless led to the belief he would relinquish his marine insurance. Mr. Wharton's business grew slowly, for a policy of his to Thomas Riché, underwritten by John Baynton, on Goods from Philadelphia to Antigua, at ten per cent., dated 25 October, 1756, is registered in his " Book B, fol. 64." In his advertisements for many years he continues his notice of an Insurance Office. In 1765 he associates with him his son, and the firm is Thomas and Isaac Wharton :

" N. B.—An Insurance Office for Shipping is Kept by them."

Pennsylvania Gazette, 30 October, 1766.

The latter, in 1781, associates with him his kinsman, Samuel Lewis Wharton, and their Register of Policies begins this year. Subsequently we find Isaac Wharton and David Lewis as Insurance Brokers at 115 south Front street, the latter gentleman afterwards being President of the Phœnix Insurance Company, and his son and grandson were successively Treasurers of The Mutual Assurance Company. In 1819 we find their successors, Thomas and John Wharton, "Insurance Brokers," tenants of The Insurance Company of North America, on the Dock street front of their property.

In 1756 Mr. Walter Shee opened an office, and advertises:

" NOTICE is hereby given, that Walter Shee, in Front street, at the corner of Chestnut-street, in Philadelphia, hath opened an office for the insurance of ships, and merchandize. All persons who want to have insurance made, may apply at said office, where all risks will be underwrote."

Pennsylvania Gazette, 23 September, 1756.

Mr. Shee was the third on the list of the first signers of the Hibernia Fire Company, 20 February, 1752.

A policy issued by him on 15 May, 1758, to Thomas Riché, on Merchandise from St. Christopher's to Philadelphia, at ten per cent., underwritten by William Moore, is registered by him in his "Book B, fol. 62," from which we may estimate the growth of his business. In 1760 he informs the public:

> " N. B.—The Insurance Office for Shipping and Merchandize is kept by him as usual."
>
> *Pennsylvania Gazette,* 6 March, 1760.

He subsequently associates with himself his brother, Bertles Shee:

> " NOW opening at their store in Front Street, five doors from the corner of Chestnut-street.
>
> "WALTER AND BERTLES SHEE."
>
> " N. B.—The Insurance office for Shipping continued by them as usual."
>
> *Pennsylvania Gazette,* 26 September, 1765.
>
> "At their store in Second street, nearly opposite the Golden Fleece Tavern."
>
> *Pennsylvania Gazette,* 7 May, 1767.

Following these, next came the office of Kidd and Bradford, located at Colonel Bradford's store in the Old London Coffee House, that ancient building at the southwest corner Front and Market streets, which remained intact up to 1883, and was announced by the following advertisement:

> Philadelphia, 8 April.
>
> NOTICE is hereby given that on *Monday* next an INSURANCE OFFICE for INSURING Shipping, and Merchandize will be opened at

the *London Coffee House*, where Risks in general will be underwrote, and all Perfons may have their Infurance made with Care and Expedition by

JOHN KIDD
and
WILLIAM BRADFORD.

Pennsylvania Journal. Tuesday, 8 April, 1762.

Colonel Bradford's paper, the *Journal*, in its issue of the following week advertised :

"*The Philadelphia* INSURANCE OFFICE is now opened adjoining the *London* Coffee House, for INSURING Shipping and Merchandize, where Risks in general will be underwrote, &c."*

But prior to Kidd and Bradford's office, a New York broker had sought for Philadelphia business, for Mr. Anthony Van Dam advertises his office in the *Pennsylvania Gazette*, 13 September, 1759, as follows :

"The New York *Insurance Office* is opened at the Houſe of the Widow Smith, adjoining the Merchants' Coffee Houſe : where all Riſks are underwrote at moderate Premiums. Constant Attendance will be given from the Hours of Eleven to One in the Forenoon, and from Six to Eight in the Evening, by Anthony Van Dam, Clerk of the Office."

Mr. Van Dam was a citizen of New York, eminent in business and social circles, one of the incorporators of the New York Chamber of Commerce under its charter of 1770, and its first Secretary, who, espousing the British side in the Revolution, went to England after its close. There were other insurance Offices in New York at the same period, but Mr. Van Dam alone extended his operations to this city. The site of his office is believed to be the modern 93 Wall street.

* Col. Bradford's eminent and useful career is faithfully portrayed in *An Old Philadelphian, Colonel William Bradford, The Patriot Printer of 1776, Sketches of his Life*, by his descendant John William Wallace, Esquire, *Philadelphia*, 1884.

Thus much for the early Brokers and their Insurance Offices. We now note the beginnings of associated underwriting. In the year 1757 certain merchants—namely, Thomas Willing, Attwood Shute, Charles Stedman, Alexander Stedman, John Kidd, and William Coxe entered into Articles of Agreement, under date of 8 October, "under the name and style of Thomas Willing and Company," for the purpose of underwriting policies of marine insurance. Their preamble recites, "Whereas the Insurance of Vessels and Merchandize has proved a great Encouragement to Trades, and that by Companies is most secure to the Insured. Therefore to establish a Company for insuring Ships, Vessels, Goods and Merchandise on reasonable terms," &c., &c. They were not to write more than £600, lawful money of Pennsylvania, nor less than £50, on any one risk, and a regular set of books were to be opened. Thomas Willing was to be the cashier, and the books kept "in the Counting House of the said Thomas Willing, in Front-Street." Each partner had one-sixth interest. New Articles of Agreement were made 20 October, 1758, by the same parties, excepting Mr. Shute, whose place was taken by Robert Morris, the same name and style continuing. No funds were put up by the partners, and the "Company" issued its policies simply upon the united credit of its partners, which assuredly made a strong guarantee of indemnity.

This effort evidenced that the practice of individual underwriting was growing here, and indeed, probably, invited it among those of our merchants whose surplus wealth was increasing. How long "Thomas Willing and

Company" continued to underwrite policies cannot now be ascertained; but as their agreements both of 1757 and 1758 were but for a twelvemonth each, no renewal may have been had in 1759.

On 20 April, 1762, Mr. John Kidd and Colonel John Nixon established a like "Company," which at its expiration the following year was renewed for another twelvemonth. Kidd and Nixon's subscriptions to policies, which were made by Colonel Nixon individually, were not to "underwrite more than two hundred pounds lawfull money of Pennsylvania upon any one bottom or risque whatever."

Merchants procured their insurances from the individual underwriters, through the instrumentality of the brokers, at whose offices risks were offered and terms arranged, and who secured the policy from those of their clients, either individual or associated, who were willing to underwrite the applicant. This class of gentlemen, which had grown in importance, in a few years claimed some compensation over and above that which might accrue upon the adjustment of losses, and we see thus early the beginning of the commission question.

On 12 February, 1762, we find there was a meeting held of sundry of our local underwriters—namely, Henry Harrison, Peter Reeve, Amos Strettle, Conyngham and Nesbitt, Scott and McMichael, Samuel Purviance, John Wilcocks, Willing, Morris and Co., Samuel Mifflin, Child and Stiles, Thos. and Wm. Lightfoot, Abram Judah, James and Drinker, Samuel Oldman, John Mifflin, Reed and Pettit, and Aquila Jones to discuss this broker question, and they agreed:

" That the several Brokers in whose offices they shall hereafter subscribe Policies shall be accountable for all the premiums arising from such subscriptions being allowed thereon by us the underwriters, a commission of one and a quarter per cent. for standing the Risques of such premiums, collecting and paying the same in the following manner :

" 1. That such Brokers shall settle each Underwriter's Account every three Months, and pay the Ballance due thereon exclusive of all premiums arising from Policys which have not been Subscribed above one month, and in the Intermediate time between such Settlements shall pay all losses due from us out of the Premiums on Policys which have been underwrote more than one month, or so far as such subscriptions extend."

But a more grievous cause of complaint grew up in the lowering of the rates of premiums, for as individual underwriting increased, the number of brokers' offices as well increased, and competition affected the standard of rates; and in this, history repeats itself in our modern business. On 6 May, 1766, a meeting of nineteen underwriters was held, who signed an agreement, which thus begins :

" The Subscribers hereunto being Convinced by sad Experience that the premiums of Insurance have of late been Inadequate to the risques underwrote in this City, and fearing that the Consequence of their continuing so will be an entire loss of so necessary and usefull a Branch of Business, as most of the present Underwriters are determined to decline the pursuit of it, unless some regulations of the premiums are made and generally agreed to : Wherefore we and each of us promise to and agree with each other :

" 1. That we will not subscribe our names to any Policy or Policies of Assurance at any less premium or Rates than are specified in the List annexed hereunto signed by the Brokers."

" 5. That if any Persons now in the practise of Underwriting in this City do refuse to sign and agree to these articles, We will not subscribe any Policy of Assurance to Cover any Ship, freight, or Goods the Property of such refusing underwriters, nor any other Policy which the said Refusing Underwriters may have signed."

" 9. We will subscribe no Policy but what comes from an Office Keeper."

The original MS. of this document, signed by the nineteen merchants, shows that more than one-half of the subscribers had subsequently erased their names, and so effectually in some instances as to forbid deciphering them now. Thus we may presume but little time elapsed before these gentlemen felt themselves too restricted by the agreement, and withdrew from it to join the general competition for insurances.

Mr. Kidd, one of the partners of "Thomas Willing and Company" of 1757 and 1758, subsequently engaged in the Insurance Brokerage, and in 1762 associated himself with Col. William Bradford, "the patriot printer of 1776," and the firm of Kidd and Bradford, before referred to, maintained their marine insurance office until 1768 or later, Bradford continuing it up to 1776 in his own name. Colonel Bradford left behind him a valuable miscellaneous collection of MSS. relating to politics and business, and it is among these in the Pennsylvania Historical Society that we find many insurance books and papers of his forerunners and of his own office, which the Society has arranged with intelligent care; the most interesting of the insurance documents being the Journal of his own underwriting accounts from 1768 to 1774.

The business of securing and placing risks among the local underwriters must have steadily grown in importance, for among the Insurance Brokers of Philadelphia a few years later we find in addition to the names already mentioned those of N. & J. Frazier, at No. 95 south Front street, afterwards Nalbro Frazier at No. 161 south Second street; Robert E. Hobart, who had an office at the City Tavern

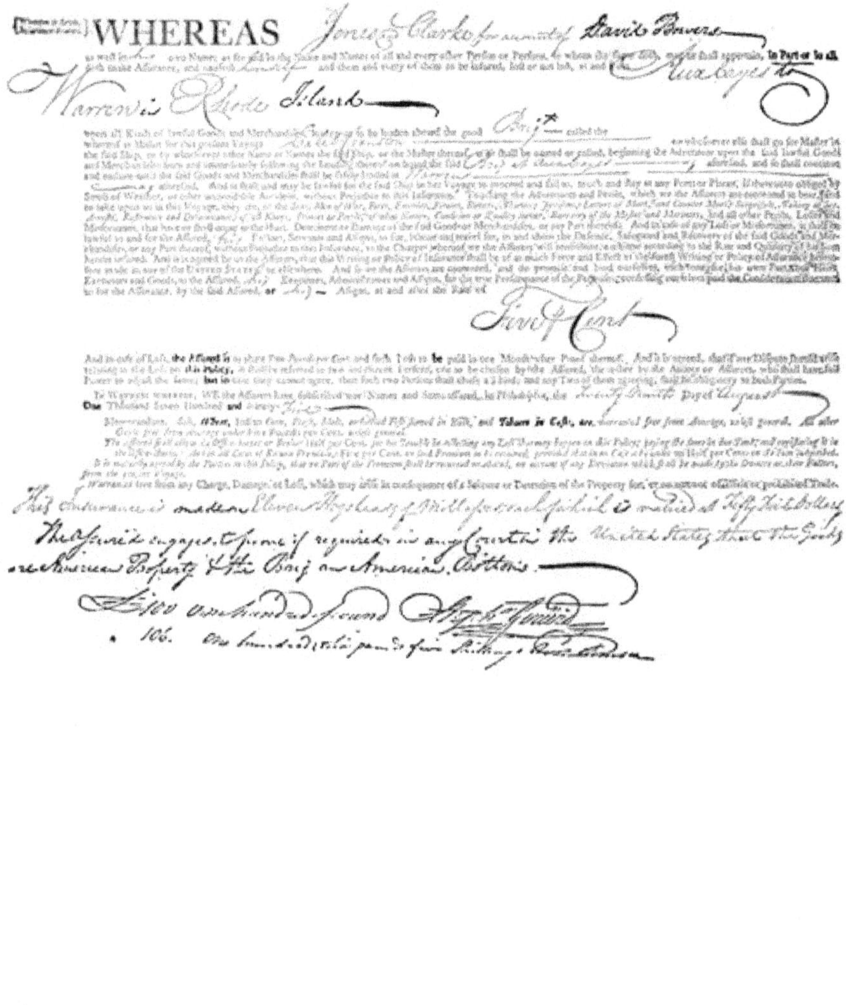

WHEREAS Jones & Clarke for account of David Bowers
Warren in Rhode Island
Five p Cent
Warranted free from any Charge, Damage, or Loss, which may arise in consequence of a Seizure or Detention of the Property for, or on account of illicit or prohibited Trade.
This Insurance is made on Eleven Hogsheads of
The Assured engages to prove if required in any Court in the United States that the Goods are American Property & the Brig an American Bottom.
£100 One hundred pounds
106. One hundred & six pounds

EARLY MARINE POLICY OF PHILADELPHIA BROKERS, 1795.

building;* Jacob Shoemaker, afterwards Shoemaker & Berrett, at No. 29 north Water street; John Donnaldson; and John Taylor, at No. 10 south Front street. Some of these gentlemen had their own policy-forms in print, with their names and office address added thereon, though the contract appears to have been the same in all cases. The modern broker is content with attaching the label of his name and address to the outside of a company's policy; those gentlemen, printing their own policy, could at once place their name and address prominently on the first page.

* Robert Enoch Hobart, the elder brother of Bishop Hobart, was an active, enterprising man, of a well-cultivated mind and literary taste. At first a merchant, then an insurance broker, he became in 1811 a resident of Batsgrove, Pennsylvania, being allied in marriage to the family on whose estate the town was built, and who gave its name; at the time of his death, he had been for two sessions a member of the State legislature.

III.

EARLY FIRE UNDERWRITING IN PHILADELPHIA.

THUS much for the growth of marine insurance in Philadelphia.

It appears to us of this day remarkable that our ancestors had no means for indemnifying themselves against losses by fire on land; no individual capitalist stood ready to underwrite indemnity to the house-owner for the possible destruction of his property by fire. Such losses, however, were not unknown to our earlier citizens, for the necessity for some mode of extinguishing fires led to the establishment of a fire company, the *Union*, on 7 December, 1736, followed by the *Fellowship*, 1 January, 1738, the *Hand-in-Hand*, 1 March, 1742, the *Heart-in-Hand*, 22 February, 1743, the *Friendship*, 30 July, 1747, and the *Hibernia*, 22 February, 1752, with an aggregate membership of two hundred and twenty-five members, employing seven engines, one thousand and fifty-five buckets, and thirty-six ladders. This force witnesses to the dangers from fire the citizens felt themselves surrounded with, and yet they remained without any source of indemnity from loss whatever, until 13 April, 1752, when certain *Contributers*, as they were called, then organized under a Deed of Settlement *The Philadelphia Contributionship for the Insurance of Houses from Loss by Fire*, and it was not until

1 June following, that any member of this mutual association sought its first policy, and he was the Hon. John Smith, the author of the "Deed of Settlement," and the first treasurer of the company.

This organization was the result of an invitation to

> "*All persons inclined to subscribe to the articles of insurance of houses from fire, in or near this city, are desired to appear at the Court-house, where attendance will be given, to take in their subscriptions every seventh day of the week, in the afternoon, until the 13th of April next, being the day appointed by the said articles for electing twelve directors and a treasurer,*"

which was first inserted in the *Pennsylvania Gazette*, on 18 February, 1752, and continued therein until the date of meeting, but the paper gives no intelligence of the action then had. The office of the company, we have already seen, was opened at the store of Mr. Joseph Saunders, its first "Clerk."

Mr. Smith was a native of Burlington, New Jersey, and a younger brother of Samuel Smith the Historian of New Jersey; he was at this period a prominent merchant in Philadelphia, and had established the first line of regular packets trading to Liverpool from this city, was a member of the General Assembly of the Province of Pennsylvania, and prominent in the affairs of the Society of Friends, and one of the originators of the Pennsylvania Hospital; he was the promoter of this invaluable scheme, and to him must be conceded the honor of its authorship. Though but thirty years of age at this time, his practical views at once enlisted Benjamin Franklin's co-operation, and this with his own personal influence in the community, which was enhanced by his being the son-in-law of James Logan,

Chief Justice and afterwards President of the Council of Pennsylvania, and whose death had occurred but a few months before, secured the establishment of the first insurance organization in the American Colonies.

He was an active member of the Hand-in-Hand fire company, then a young organization, which he joined shortly upon his coming to Philadelphia in 1743, and which in time enrolled in its membership some of the leading citizens, and in its later history, continued the same characteristics of membership. In the year 1771 the entire corporation of the city, according to Mr. Thompson Westcott, appears to have been embraced in its membership, and statesmen, lawyers, physicians, divines and merchants were among its "honorablemen"; four signers of the Declaration of Independence, Clymer, Hopkinson, Rush and Wilson, Chief Justice Tilghman, Bishop White, Provost Smith, long maintained their membership. In later years it ceased active duties at fires, fulfilling only its social claims in the monthly dinners, and leaving the use of its engine to other organizations, and finally ceased to exist in 1817; of its last roll of members, the Hon. Horace Binney was one. Mr. Smith in his MS. Journal, before referred to, makes frequent allusions to attendance on its meetings; and his connection with it may have secured his attention to some scheme of insuring owners of buildings from loss by fire. On 26 August, 1748, his Journal records: "in the evening rode to Stenton; took with me a plan of the damage done by the fire in London, and gave to the old gentleman; and the magazines for March and April, which I left with Hannah." This reference is to the fire on 25 March preceding, which consumed two hundred houses in Cornhill, the severest conflagration in London since the great fire of 1666 (Walford's *Cyclopædia*). The Journal unhappily ends before the establishment of the Contributionship, but from the entry now quoted, we can judge that the thought of such a company, and perhaps its plan of organization, were the result of mature consideration before he presented the subject to the citizens of Philadelphia. While its popular title *Hand-in-Hand* "is not contained in any part of the Deed of Settlement, nor in the policy, nor in any of its minute-books or papers" (Mr. Binney's *Centennial Address*, page 29), we cannot but connect its use from the outset with the title of Mr. Smith's fire company, many of the members of this, being the contributors in that.

A later by-law of the Contributionship forbade the insurance on buildings surrounded by trees, which was expressly permitted by its Deed of Settlement; this led to the formation on 5 July, 1784 of the *Mutual Assurance Company for Insuring Houses from Loss by Fire in and near Philadelphia*, to whom our citizens by the payment of an additional Deposit could have both their Insurances and their Trees.

The interest and feeling created by this restriction in the Contributionship Articles can best be seen in the public announcement made by the objectors, which we find in their advertisement in the *Gazette* of 25 August, 1784:

Philadelphia, August 10, 1784.
A NEW SOCIETY
For insuring Houses from Loss by Fire.

A GREAT number of the citizens of Philadelphia, who are proprietors of houses in the city and its suburbs, many of whom now are or have been Members of *the Philadelphia Contributionship for insuring Houses from Lofs by Fire*, have found it convenient and agreeable to them to have trees planted in the ftreets before their houfes, which the said *Contribution-fhip* have thought proper to prohibit by one of their bye-laws, although the same is expressly permitted by a law of the State, and notwithftanding application has been made by above forty of their Members to have the faid bye-law repealed, who fignified their willingnefs that an addition fhould be made to the premium of their insurance for the fuppofed rifque attending trees in cafes of fire, as is now done with refpect to bake-houfes, coopers, apothecaries and oil men's fhops, ftores containing pitch, tar, brimstone, &c., which application has been rejected.

Wherefore a number of perfons, desirous of having their houfes infured from lofs by fire, and feeing themfelves precluded from the advantages of the prefent inftitution, have judged it necessary to form another fociety for the purpofe aforefaid, and have entered into an agreement, that as foon as fo many perfons as have property in houfes to the value of one Hundred Thoufand Pounds collectively, shall have figned the faid agreement, a meeting of the fubscribers fhould be called, to form a plan for the management of the intended fociety.

That having no intention to prejudice the inftitution already eftablifhed, and being only actuated by a defire to fecure their own property, they further agreed, that if the bye-law above referred to shall be repealed within ten months from the date of their agreement, which was the 5th of July, 1784, that then their faid agreement fhould be void, or otherwife to be carried into execution.

Subfcriptions to near the amount above prescribed having already been made, at a meeting of the fubscribers it was unanimoufly agreed to lay their proceedings before the public, and to inform fuch as are difpofed to join them, that fubfcription papers are lodged with Mr. WILLIAM CRAIG, in Second-ftreet, and Mr. JOHN PHILIPS, at the corner of Front and Pine-ftreets.

A meeting of the fubscribers will be held in September next, whereof each one will be informed by a particular notice.

In the *Gazette* of 27 October, 1784, we find the following:

The Office of the Mutual Affurance
Company, for infuring Houfes from lofs by Fire,

IS kept by the fubscriber, at his houfe in Quarry-ftreet, between Moravian-alley and Third-ftreet, where the members of the said Company and all others defirous of having their property infured may apply.

APPLICATIONS will also be received at the store of Mr. MATTHEW CLARKSON, in Front-ftreet, between Market and Arch-ftreets.

John Jennings, Clerk.

By the President and Directors of the Insurance Company of North America.

WHEREAS *Anthony Butler of the District of the Northern Liberties*

hath paid to the President and Directors of the Insurance Company of North America ... Dollars, for Insurance of ...

No 6

2000 Two thousand Dollars

Dwelling House No. 2000 —

EARLY FIRE POLICY ON BUILDING, 1795.

Article XXXII of their Deed of Settlement is as follows:

> "That there be an Addition to the Deposite Money upon the Insurance of all Houses having Trees planted before them, and also for Trees planted in Yards near the Houses; which Addition shall be determined by the *Trustees*, and be in proportion to the Risque such Trees may occasion. All Trees planted near Houses shall be Trimmed every Fall, in such Manner as not to he higher than the Eaves of the Houses. And Trees planted after Insurance made must be reported to the Office, and the additional Deposite paid within twelve Months after they are planted, or the Deposite Money will be forfeited and the Insurance become Void."

One practical result arises from this favor, interesting to the arboriculturist, by often establishing the date of the shade trees planted by our old citizens; one instance we find at Bishop White's dwelling, built by him in 1786, No. 89 (now 309) Walnut street, for not until 14 November, 1795, did he plant his trees, as we find by endorsement on his Policy No. 191, he made "his Deposite for Planting two Trees in front of the within described house and paid to the Treasurer one pound five shillings," which was at the rate of one-quarter of one per cent. for the privilege of shade trees.

This Company became and still is popularly known as the *Green Tree*, from the house badge it adopted, as the Contributionship, from its early badge of four-clasped hands is as well known by the name of the *Hand-in-Hand*. The latter's office, at the time of the organization of the Insurance Company of North America, was kept in the house of its "Clerk," Mr. Caleb Carmalt (afterwards Treasurer from 1807 to 1817), located at No. 99 (now 239)

a

Market street; and the former at No. 92 (now 230) Vine street, the residence of its Clerk, Mr. John Jennings; both the buildings thus occupied have now disappeared, and modern structures stand in their places.

In General Assembly,

TUESDAY, *April* 2, 1793.

An ACT *to incorporate the* Insurance Society Company *of* North America.

1 Whereas a Company has been formed in the city of Philadel-
2 phia and a competent capital thereto subscribed for the purpose of car-
3 rying on the business of insurance and application has been made to the
4 Legislature by the said Company for an act of incorporation In
5 order therefore to promote an institution which by alleviating the
6 risques and losses incident to trade and navigation must in its operations
7 be equally beneficial to the agricultural and commercial interests of the
8 state.

1 Sect. 1. *Be it enacted by the Senate and House of Representatives*
2 *of the Commonwealth of Pennsylvania in General Assembly met and it is*
3 *hereby enacted by the authority of the same* That the capital Stock
4 of the Insurance Company of North America may amount to
5 any sum not exceeding six hundred thousand dollars that the same shall
6 be divided into sixty thousand shares of ten dollars each share and that
7 the persons copartnerships or bodies politic who have thereto subscribed
8 shall pay the residue of the sum and sums of money due and payable
9 for the share or shares by them respectively subscribed in the manner

following

IV.

INCORPORATION.

WITH this review of the early schemes of underwriting in Philadelphia, there can be formed some idea of the extent in which individual capital was interested in ventures by sea, and how favorably was received on its announcement, the plan of organization in which those seeking the uncertain profit of underwriting, could become shareholders in a reputable institution, and leave the direction and character of their ventures to a Board composed of responsible and intelligent gentlemen.

The new Board of the Insurance Company of North America met the day following their election, 11 December, 1792, at the City Tavern, that well-known place of resort in those days, which was situated on the west side of Second street, north of Walnut, on whose site was afterwards erected the Bank of Pennsylvania, now in its turn displaced by the Government Warehouse, which covers the entire lot between Second street and Dock street, and Gold and Lodge alleys. All the Directors were present, and Mr. John Maxwell Nesbitt was unanimously chosen President, and Mr. Ebenezer Hazard, Secretary; and the Directors divided themselves by lot into committees of two. Gen. Stewart, Mr. Moylan and Mr. Ball were appointed a com-

mittee to petition the Legislature for a charter, and prepare
a bill for that purpose; and the Secretary was directed to
prepare a draft of a marine policy for their consideration.
Messrs. Ross, Pettit and Miller were a committee to make
a table of the lowest premiums as a guide to the sitting
committees; and Mr. Ross, Major Moore and Mr. Leamy,
a committee to provide suitable offices for temporary
accommodation of the Company, and were authorized to
make such arrangements, with the approbation of the
President.

On Friday, 14 December, the Board met at six o'clock,
P. M., in their own offices in the brick building No. 119
(now 213) south Front street, which they leased to 1 May,
1794, at £100 per annum, from Mr. Thomas Mackie, who
occupied the building, which was owned by Mr. John
Mifflin. On the day following, 15 December, their first
Policies were issued.

Gen. Stewart's committee, under their instructions, prepared a petition to the Legislature, and three copies of the
Memorial were made, each signed by all the Directors
respectively for the Governor, the Senate, and the House.
Messrs. Stewart, Moylan and Miller were appointed to
carry it to the Governor; Messrs. Moore, Leamy and
Cramond, to the Senate, and Messrs. Barclay, Ross and
Pettit to the House. Its text is important as showing
in a formal manner the substantial reasons for the chartered establishment of such an institution, and is as
follows:

> To the Honorable the REPRESENTATIVES of the FREEMEN of the Common-
> wealth of PENNSYLVANIA in General Assembly met, The petition of the

Directors of the Insurance Company of North America, *in behalf of the said Company,* MOST RESPECTFULLY SHEWETH

That your petitioners, attached to the public welfare, behold with the greatest satisfaction the commercial pursuits and interests of the United States becoming daily more numerous and important; but they have long regretted that, for want of sufficient number of underwriters of responsibility in the principal cities and towns of the United States, commerce is burthened with the charge of commissions to European correspondents for effecting insurances, and large sums of money are consequently drained from the country.

That these considerations have induced a number of the citizens of this Commonwealth to raise a fund for the purpose of insurance and to associate themselves under the name and title of *The Insurance Company of North America,* upon the principles contained in a plan which they have the honor with this memorial to submit to your perusal.

That your petitioners humbly conceive that considerable benefits will result from this association as well to the citizens of this commonwealth in general, as to the mercantile part of this community in particular, by retaining in the State the money invested in their capital stock and the large sums that must otherwise be drawn from the country for premiums of insurance, by relieving commerce from the present tribute paid to foreign underwriters, and by securing the assured through the means of an ample capital stock from a possibility of loss, which in the manner of making insurances heretofore practised both frequently happened through the failure of individual underwriters.

The whole number of shares into which the capital stock of the company is divided, being already subscribed, the association are prepared to enter upon the prosecution of their intended object; but in order to establish a greater confidence in the minds of persons who may incline to do business with them, and to enable the assured, in case of disputed losses, to have more convenient recourse to law, as well as to enable the company to prosecute their undertaking with greater ease and effect, your petitioners are advised to apply to the Legislature for an act of incorporation.

Your petitioners, therefore, confiding, from your experienced patriotism, that every opportunity to advance the opulence, the ease, and independence of the citizens, will be cheerfully embraced, pray your aid in the premises, and permission to bring in a bill of incorporation for the purposes aforesaid.

This with the accompanying form of Constitution, drafted by Alexander James Dallas, were presented in person to the House and Senate on Tuesday the 18th December, and the next day the Memorial was read twice and referred to a Committee consisting of Messrs. Swanwick, Forrest, Turner, Eyerly, and Gallatin to make report thereon.

Opposition, however, was soon presented to their project, for on the 29th, "a petition from a number of the merchants and insurers of the port of Philadelphia was read remonstrating against the prayer contained in the petition of the Directors of the Insurance Company of North America," which on 3 January, 1793, was read twice and referred to the same committee. This was met on the 12th by "Memorials from a number of the merchants, Ship owners, Insurers, and citizens of the port of Philadelphia, praying that the Company stiling themselves the Insurance Company of North America may be incorporated," which were on the 14th in turn referred to the Committee; and these were followed on 5th February by another petition to like effect. The month passed without any action by the House, nor did the Committee submit their views; and on 28 February, the Directors appointed Gen. Stewart and Messrs. Blodget and Ralston a Committee to memorialize the Legislature of Delaware for an Act of Incorporation, and to draft a Bill for the same; but the Journals of the Delaware Assembly give no evidence that a memorial reached that body.

This move of the Directors, and which they did not conceal, brought from the Committee on 11 March a favorable report to the House, in which is disclosed the motives of

the opposition, and consequently merits here a perusal, and
is as follows:

That they confider the welfare and profperity of the agricultural
interest of the State, as infeparably connected with that of its commerce and navigation.

That no commerce or navigation could be beneficially conducted without infurance, no body chusing to commit confiderable property to the
ocean, without guarding against the numerous accidents to which it would
be thereby expofed.

That infurance cannot be fo well conducted by individuals as by an
incorporated company, for want of that identity that would enable such
a company to be fued in cafe of lofs, where juftice could be had much
more fpeedily than in fuing every feparate underwriter to a policy, a
work of fuch immenfe expence and lofs of time, as frequently to defeat
entirely the object of infurance.

That folidity is alfo to be confidered, which it is impoffible to attain
with certainty with private underwriters, whereas this Company's pro-
pofed capital of 600,000 dollars in the public funds, will be a fufficient
guarantee to thofe who employ them.

That already the charges of infurance have been confiderably abated
since the eftablishment of this company, whereby a great faving to the
mercantile body is effected, who can afford to give fo much more for the
produce, as they pay lefs for infuring it.

That the number of perfons underwriting in *Philadelphia*, does not at
prefent exceed about fifty, and the risques they take, being on an average
only about £200, on a single bottom, of courfe only about £10,000 can
now be infured at the different offices here on a single risque, which
occafions a drain of money for infurance to Europe, or to the neighboring
States, very prejudicial to the body of this one.

That it is not in the contemplation of the petitioners to exact or ask
for themselves any exclusive privilege of infurance, fo that thofe private
underwriters, or any others, may ftill go on to infure, as heretofore, for
thofe who will employ them; confequently that only a competition on a
more enlarged fcale will enfue very beneficially to the carrying on of the
businefs in queftion.

That in almost all commercial countries fimilar incorporations exist;
that in our own there are such for infuring houfes from loss by fire, it

would not be eafy to fhew why the prefent Company fhould not be incorporated on the same or like principles.

For thefe reasons the Committee fubmit the following refolution:

Refolved, That leave be given to the petitioners to bring in a bill conformably to the prayer of their petition.

On the 30th of March, this report was taken up for a second reading, and the Resolution adopted, and on the 1st of April the bill was reported, but on the 11th, the Assembly adjourned. The opposition of the private underwriters had thus prevailed effectually to postpone an early incorporation, for a chartered organization threatened their own continuance in business, and their profits had already been diminished by a reduction in premiums.

But the payment by the Directors of a six per cent. dividend on the paid subscriptions on the capital in the following July, threw the opposition on another plan of attack, for the pecuniary success of the Company had been so great and rapid as to lead its opponents to depreciate the chartering of only one such organization, and they hastened to appeal that the Directors of the North America should not be the only favored ones; and the contest remained on this ground at the following annual session of the Legislature. On 9 December, 1793, the Directors recorded a minute, "That the Directors take opportunities of conversing with the City members of Assembly to gain their interest in favor of our application for a charter," and on the following day the bill was reported to the House among the unfinished business of the former session, and on the 11th was referred to the City members Messrs. Hiltzheimer, Latimer, Swanwick, B. R. Morgan and Kammerer.

492. John Ely Fifty shares

671. Dominick Lynch of New York by by John O'Connor One hundred Shares

494 Robt. Smock Forty Shares.

495 Franc Ingraham Fifty Shares

496 Wm Burrows Ten shares

497 John Swanwick by Edward Fox one hundred shares

498 James Chatworth Ten shares

499 Jas Smith Ten Shares

500 Willie Murray Thirteen shares
501. Ebenezer Karsad for Tench Francis Twenty five Shares

502 Isaac Norris for Thomas Buckley Three Shares

503. James Wills ten shares

504. John Rutgers twenty shares

505. Joseph Byrnes Twenty Shares

506 Paul Cox Two shares

507. Wm Bingham Fifty Shares

508 Lloyd Wharton Twenty Shares

509 Thos Bates Two Shares

511 Wm McPherson Thirty Shares

510 Alexander Henry One hundred

535 Waller & John Pharies Ten shares

512 Saml Soams Fifty shares

513. William Crosman ten shares

514 James Cranford Ninety Shares

515 Thos Wheatley Fifty Shares

516 for Peter Cranford one hundred shares

517 Sam Willis ten shares

518 Joseph Thompson Ten shares

On the 13th the Directors again memorialised the House, and on the 16th "the petitions for and against read in the last House," were now again read and referred to the same committee, to which were added Messrs. Magoffin and Jacob Morgan. Another six per cent. dividend in January added force to the struggle, and delay yet held the day. On the 20 January, 1794, Messrs. Pettit, Stewart, West, Ralston and Forde were appointed to wait on the members of Assembly to urge the passage of the bill, doubtless foreseeing the renewed attempt to thwart their plans, for on the 27th "a petition from divers merchants of the City of Philadelphia was read, suggesting the impropriety of incorporating the present subscribers to the Insurance Company of North America, and praying, that should the Legislature deem it proper to pass an Act for the incorporation of an Insurance Company, the same may be done in such manner, as that those who are more immediately interested in commerce may have an opportunity of subscribing thereto, under such regulations as the Legislature have heretofore directed with respect to other incorporated Companies." This was read a second time the following day and was referred to the Philadelphia members, and on the 31st, they reported favorably. The report of the Committee is long, but forms an interesting document, amplifying the statements presented by the Committee of the previous session as to the value and need of sound and responsible indemnity in a mercantile community like Philadelphia. Portions of it are entitled to a place here.

* * * * As it is impoſſible for a merchant, with ſafety, to hazard, unprotected, his property, on ſo uncertain an element as water, which is ſo liable to prejudice or endanger it, it becomes eſſential to the farmer, miller, or manufacturer, that he ſhould inſure it.

Inſurance is an undertaking on the part of one or more individuals, in proportion to the ſums they reſpectively take or ſubſcribe, to bear harmleſs the merchant in this export trade.

This inſurance is effected in two ways, one by private aſſurers, and theſe give perſonal ſecurity only for what they undertake; the other is by public companies, and theſe mortgage a public and known capital for their tranſactions.

The cheaper inſurance is done, the better price the farmer or manufacturer will obtain; for this being one of the charges in transportation of the ſurplus, it muſt, of courſe, be underſtood or reckoned in the valuation of it.

*   *   *   *   *   *   *   ::   *

Private underwriters only afford a precarious dependence in a country; it expoſes the trade to depend too much on the fears or caprice of a few individuals; their ſecurity alſo being perſonal only, is uncertain—and in case of great events or loſſes, as has often been experienced, it proves inadequate to the occaſion.

Public underwriters only would be dangerous as a monopoly, though the ſecurity be more perfect from the capital depoſited. It therefore reſults that a wiſe government ought to encourage both theſe claſſes of aſſurers; to act in competition with each other with the aſſured, it remains which he will prefer.

*   *   *   *   *   *   *   *   *

If, therefore, the public company offers a large and known depoſit for security, in lieu of private reſponſibility, it is for the benefit of the public to accept the compromiſe, inaſmuch as a known depoſit or mortgage, is better than a precarious perſonal reſponſibility, ſubject to so many viciſſitudes.

If, therefore, the companies for inſurance prayed for be incorporated, it is obvious that all private underwriters are free as before to underwrite, but a new capital is ſuperadded to make new inſurances by the company, and that which augments the quantity of any beneficial kind of labor, cannot but of neceſſity be uſeful.

If the profits ſhould be great, new companies will ariſe to ſhare them, and as no exclusive privilege is granted, the Legiſlature may always countenance such new undertakings, when they find the proposals engaging.

For these reasons the committee are of opinion it will be advantageous for the community to incorporate, on suitable conditions, the Insurance Company of *North America*, as from their meritorious exertions during the late hazardous periods of war and foreign risque, the commerce of this and other States have been materially benefited by the exertions of the company ; but as a number of the ship owners and traders of *Philadelphia*, from local circumstance, have not been able to obtain shares in this company, and there is reason to believe that more than one company may be employed at the present period of difficulty to American commerce to much advantage, and greatly to the security and emolument thereof ; therefore your committee recommend the following resolutions to be adopted by the House, viz. :

Resolved, That a Committee be appointed to bring in a bill to incorporate the Insurance Company of *North America*, now existing in this city, for the purposes prayed for.

Resolved, That a Committee be also appointed to bring in a bill for organizing and establishing a new Insurance Company in the said city of *Philadelphia*, to be carried on under the firm or denomination of " The Insurance Company of the State of *Pennsylvania*."

Thus was originated the second Stock Insurance Company in the Commonwealth.

On the 1st of February this report was read a second time and a committee appointed, viz.: Messrs. Hiltzheimer, Swanwick, B. Morgan and Kammerer, to bring in a bill, which, however, they did not report until the 22d, with one also for the State of Pennsylvania. From this date there seemed to be an effort, by moving amendments to the former, to delay it, and the latter passed the House on the 13th March, while the North America reached its passage on the 14th. The bills reached the Senate in like order, and on the 20th they were both made the order for the 26th. The North America charter secured the precedence, and on

the 28th it passed with a few amendments, and sent to the
House, which concurred on the 1st of April. The State of
Pennsylvania bill reached its passage on the 3d of April.
The former was signed by Governor Mifflin on the 14th,
and the latter by him on the 18th of April.

The bare legislative record of this struggle can only afford
glimpses of the ardor with which the contest was continued
against the new enterprise, first on one ground of opposition
and then on another; but the two incorporations, born of
the contest, have honorably stood side by side without a
memory of the work of 1793, and have passed through
together many a crisis of underwriting and still live to show
the strength of their Constitutions.

Section 4 of the Charter provided for twenty-five
Directors, "and that in case any Director shall be chosen
a Director of any other Insurance Company and shall act
as such," his place was declared vacant. To this condition
was due the loss from time to time of some influential
Directors, who, becoming interested in new organizations,
gave their energies to planting them, at the loss of their
official connection with the older corporation. Thus on 13
November, 1794, Messrs. Archibald McCall and Thomas
Fitzsimons, being elected to the Direction of the Insurance
Company of the State of Pennsylvania, their places were
declared vacant; and on 1 August, 1803, Mr. Ball, the
former President, Commodore Dale, Mr. Lewis Clapier, and
others, became thus ineligible and their places declared
vacant, the three gentlemen named having become interested
in the new Union Insurance Company just incorporated.
On 28 January, 1813, on which occasion the President and

Mr. Henry went to Harrisburg, sundry amendments were made, one reducing the number of Directors to fifteen, and another granting an enlargement of the field for investment, when an extension was granted to 1 January, 1835. On 3 April, 1833, an extension of the charter was granted for twenty years from the last limit named; and on 11 October, 1839, the same was made perpetual, with a view to write perpetual risks. By Act of 6 April, 1842, consent was given to reduction of the capital to $300,000 the par value of shares being five dollars. On 11 February, 1845, a new supplement authorized an increase in the number of Directors to twenty, without repealing the condition above recited of 14 April, 1794, which was repeated in the supplement of 28 January, 1813. By Act of 8 May, 1850, authority was granted to restore the Capital to the extent of five hundred thousand dollars and the par value of the shares to ten dollars. On 27 February, 1854, authority was given the Company "to appoint agents or officers, effect insurances in any of the other States of the Union or without its limits, and that contracts of insurance effected by such agents or officers, shall be as valid and binding as if the same were effected by the President and Directors." On 14 March, 1871, authority was given to increase the capital to one million dollars and the par value of the shares of stock to twenty dollars; and this supplement repeated the powers of the company in marine, fire, and life insurances, as recited in section third of the original act. The supplement of 1 May, 1876, to an act to establish an Insurance Department (of 4 April, 1873), permitting any existing company to increase its capital stock by vote of

Stockholders. providing the same be certified to the Insurance Commissioner: the Company accepted at a meeting of Stockholders held 10 July following, and under the conditions of the supplement, their action had "the same force and effect as if a part of the Company's original charter or constituting a supplement thereto"; and forthwith the capital was doubled, making it two million dollars. And on the 15 November, 1880, a further increase of one million dollars was made, the shares being allotted to Stockholders at a premium of ten dollars each: the Directors believing that the soundest extension of the Company's means was by an equal increase of its capital and its reserve.

Philadelphia

1792
Sitting Committee, Mess.rs Mc.Connal & Ball

Dec.r 15.th Policy N.o 1.

Wrote for Conyngham, Nesbett & C.o
at ⅞ from Philadelphia to Londonderry,
on the Ship America, James Ewing M.r
valued at Twelve Thousand Dollars
5.333.33 Doll.s @ 2¼ ⅌C.t — — — — — 120.—
Policy — — —.50

Doll.s | C.t
.120..50

Dec.r 15.th Policy N.o 2.

Wrote for Conyngham, Nesbitt & C.o
at ⅞ from Phil.a to Londonderry, on Goods
on board the Ship America, James
Ewing Master
3200 Doll.s @ 2¼ ⅌C.t — — — — — 72.—
Policy — — — —.50

.. 72..50

Dec.r 15.th Policy N.o 3.

Wrote for John Leamy, at &
from Phil.a to New Orleans, with Liberty
to touch & trade at Caper Francois, on
Goods on board the Brig Margarita
Anthony Arnaud, Master
1500 Dollars @ 3 ⅌C.t — — — — — 45.—
Policy — — — —.50

.. 45..50

Dec.r 15.th Policy N.o 4.

Wrote for Stuart & Barr, (at: &
from Alexandria in Virginia to
Falmouth in Great Britain, to trade
between Europe (without the Streights)
& America; for nine Months, com-
:mencing this Day, & to continue until
the Ship's Arrival at any safe Port
in the United States, after the Expi-
:ration of the said nine months)
on the Ship Friendship, Samuel
Hubbel.

V.

MARINE BUSINESS.

IN THE meanwhile, the business of the Company had grown rapidly, unaffected by the want of early success in obtaining a charter. The stated committees of the Board sat regularly to pass upon all applications. Mr. Hazard had opened the books and wrote the first policies, and in a few days a clerk was voted him, Mr. William Coulthard being appointed at five hundred dollars per annum. A porter was engaged, John Valentine Cline, for "£6 per month and an hint of a douceur at Christmas." And before the month was out another clerk, John Cook, was appointed. In the following March, Samuel Young was appointed Surveyor.

The first policy was issued to Conyngham, Nesbitt & Co., on the ship *America*, James Ewing, Master, from Philadelphia to Londonderry, for $5,333.33, at $2\frac{1}{4}$ per cent.; and the second on goods in same ship, for $3,200. Policy No. 3 was to John Leamy on goods on board the brig *Margarita*, Anthony Arnaud, Master, from Philadelphia to New Orleans, with liberty to touch and trade at Cape Francois, for $1,500, at 3 per cent. Policy No. 10 on the 15th was to the President, Directors and Company of the Bank of the United States, on cash laden after the 10th inst. on board any vessel, any Master, from Charleston,

South Carolina to Philadelphia or New York, for $20,000, at 1 per cent.

The form of policy employed was that in use by the local underwriters at the time. Mr. Hazard writing at the head in the usual blank, the name of the underwriter:

"The Afsurance Company of North America."

The Committee on Policy reported later a recommendation to delay printing their own until the result was known of their application for a charter. The first six months showed the premiums received $62,114.33, and premiums determined $8,910.19. The first loss was the ship *Industry*, amounting to $4,000, which was paid 10 June, and a few days later their second claim was met, $515.74, on the sloop *Betsey*. The interest account amounted to $3,276.20, and early in July the first dividend was declared and paid to stockholders, being six per cent. on the first and second instalments of the paid capital, and which amounted to $7,975.28. The second six months' premium receipts were $151,350.98, and the determined premiums, $69,184.21; interest was $3,574.41, and the losses amounted to $19,474.64. The second dividend was realized to the stockholders in January, 1794, being six per cent on the first, second and third instalments of the paid capital, amounting to $14,400. With these satisfactory returns to the stockholders, the motive for the change of base of the opponents of the company's incorporation can be seen; and as the profits of an organized business of underwriting were so manifest, these opponents were now only too eager to share in them, and instead of thwarting the desired incorporation, only asked that they also might be incorporated.

A form of marine policy for their own use appears to have been considered on 27 March, 1793, and was submitted to Messrs. Jared Ingersoll and William Tilghman, two gentlemen learned in the law, for their opinion whether it would secure the property of the individual members (other than their interest in the company's funds) from legal claims for losses; but conclusions on this do not appear to have been reached until after incorporation, as a form for the company's policy was only finally agreed to on 9 May, 1794, and at the same meeting "the Draft of a Device for Seal, presented by Mr. Blodget, was approved of." This seal remains unchanged to this time.

It had not been long before the brokers found their clients preferred the solidity of a wealthy association preferable to the credit of an individual underwriter, and brought their applications to the company claiming a commission thereon; but the board on 27 March, 1793, declined to " write for the private offices and allow the brokers two and a half per cent., they guarantying the premiums"; and realizing its strength, made public advertisement of their rules, and invited orders to be addressed directly to the company.

The following were adopted at the same meeting when the form of policy was adopted, as the "rules to be observed in transacting business with the Insurance Company of North America":

"1. All orders for Insurance must be given in writing. signed by the Applicant; and as minute a Description of the

4

Vessel is expected as the person ordering the Insurance can give, respecting her Age, Build, how found and fitted, and whether double or single decked.

"2. All Policies will be ready for Delivery in Twenty-four hours after the order for Insurance is accepted at the office, and the Policy must be taken up in Ten Days.

"3. Notes with an approved Endorser for all Premiums must be given in Ten Days, payable as follows:

" For American and West Indian Risques, in Three Months after the Date of Policy.

" For European Risques, in Six Months.

" For Indian and China Risques, in Twelve Months.

" For Risques by the Year, in Eight Months.

" For Risques for any lesser Time, in Three Months.

"4. Losses will be paid in Ten Days after Proof and Adjustment; but if the Note given for the Premium shall not have become due within that Time, the amount of it shall nevertheless be deducted from the Loss to be paid."

Their advertisement gave "notice to all whom it may concern, that agreeably to the above rules they are ready to receive all orders for Insurance which may be addressed to them, accompanied with Directions to some responsible House in Philadelphia, for the payment of the Premiums within the time limited. In case the Risques offered shall be approved, the Insurance shall be immediately effected, otherwise notice shall be given either by answer to the Person applying, or his agent in Philadelphia, as may be ordered."

By the President and Directors of the Insurance Company of North America.

No. 2639

WHEREAS *Jonathan Mifflin* ...

Philadelphia to Barbadoes & Martinique, with liberty to proceed to any other Port or Ports in the West Indies (British or Neutral) & at & from thence back to Philadelphia ...

Brig called the Sally ...

Philadelphia ...

Philadelphia ...

Himself ...

Two Ports, and the Assured agrees to pay an additional premium of one per cent for each Port the said Vessel shall proceed to or touch at more than two ...

The Assured warrants the above Goods to be American property and the Vessel an American Bottom.

$. 2686.— *Two thousand six hundred & eighty six Dollars*

Cha. Pettit Presd. pro Tem.

Dollars 2636.— on Goods, 268. 60
Policy — 50
269 10

On 8 July it was "Agreed, That Notes be received for
Premiums to New Orleans, payable in Four and an half
months." On 20 January, 1794, finding that policies were
not always paid for promptly, the board ordered "in order
the more certainly to enforce the payment of Premiums in
due Season, no Policy be subscribed by the President until
the Premium is paid, or a note given for the same in the
accustomed manner." And with the precision of banking
rules on discounts, they ordered "That all Inquiries for Insurances left at this office before 12 o'clock in the morning
shall be answered at or before three o'clock on the same
Day, and all Inquiries left after Three o'clock and before
Six o'clock, shall receive an answer at or before Ten o'clock
on the succeeding Day."

The matter of office hours was considered on 15 January,
1795, and it was resolved,

"That the office shall be open for the Transaction of
Business from Nine O'clock in the morning to Two in the
Afternoon; and from Four in the Afternoon til Eight in
the Evening. That the attendance of the Secretary be
required from Ten to Two, and from Four to Eight in the
afternoon. That it shall be the Duty of the President to
attend this office every Day from Eleven O'clock in the
Forenoon until Two o'clock in the afternoon, and from Five
o'clock in the afternoon until Eight o'clock. And that it
shall be the Duty of the Committee of the Week to attend
every day from Twelve o'clock until Two in the afternoon,
and from Six till Eight o'clock."

And in regard to applications for insurance the rules of
the previous January were affirmed.

On 2 March, 1795, "on the question shall so large a Sum as $35,000 be taken in future on Risques of the first Dignity, it was unanimously agreed in the affirmative"; showing the extent to which the policies of the company were sought by the large shippers of the country. On 8 May, 1809, the lines had been increased to $40,000.

The difficulty of investing the accumulating funds of the company led to the question of loaning on Respondentia, which was reported favorably upon by a committee on 17 November, 1794; and on 16 March following, on receipt of an application for such a loan from Captain Tingey, the board decided unanimously to make such loans, and on the 30th "it was agreed that five thousand dollars should be lent to Capt. Tingey on Respondentia, at Eighteen Months' credit, at twenty-five per cent. (including premium of insurance) for the eighteen months." A form for Respondentia Bond was approved 13 April. On 21 May the President and Committee of the Week were authorized "to write open policies in cases in which they may judge it expedient, and at such a premium as they shall think adequate to the risk." By the minutes of 8 May, 1809, the loans on Respondentia were limited to $20,000. The amount of this business was not large in the course of years, and proved unprofitable in the aggregate, and was finally declined altogether.

The success of the company during its early years was certainly remarkable considering the period, for its beginning was during the time of bitter warfare between Great Britain and France, when both parties made free on the high seas with any property afloat upon which they could make any claim. "Our vessels began to be boarded and captured by the various parties engaged in the great European struggle, and most of all by France, who mindless of her Treaty of Alliance with us [6 February, 1778], as well as of the Treaty of Amity and Commerce, which was concluded upon the same day, entered upon a systematic course of capture and confiscation." *   General Washington's proclamation of neutrality of 22 April, 1793, was the inciting cause to the depredations of the French on our commerce, as they claimed our neutrality was in violation of the treaty of 1778. So severe losses had already been experienced by our shippers, that in less than a year, on 27 August, 1793, they were invited by the Secretary of State, to throw their claims in the hands of the government, and trust to it for redress. The drain on the company's resources became heavy from these causes, yet they continued to take the increased hazards, hoping an end might be reached to the struggle. In those days of slow communications, they were earning heavy losses by both British and French cruisers, and many months would elapse before the tidings reached the office, and in the meanwhile they were issuing policies which in turn might realize to them accumulating losses. The alarm of the board first finds expression on 12 October, 1795, when it was "resolved, that Messrs. Ralston, Fry and Smith wait on the Secretary of State and inform him that a Report prevails that the French cruisers have orders to Capture all vessels bound to British Ports and request him to apply to the French minister to know whether this is so or not." On the 29 February following,

---

* Address prepared by Messrs. Wallis, Macalester and Hilton, by order of the Convention of Claimants, held in New York, 13 October, 1856.

Messrs. Ball, Fry and Ralston were appointed a "Committee to arrange and state the claims of this company against the Government of Great Britain, and the Captor or others, into whose hands the Property may have came, in cases of Capture and Depredation in the American Trade, so far as concerns this Company, to consult Counsel thereon if they find it expedient, and devise the proper mode of prosecuting our claims arising thereon, either through the Intervention of the Government of the United States or otherwise." On 16 April a committee was appointed to confer with the Insurance Company of the State of Pennsylvania and the private underwriters who had appointed committees to meet and consider what steps are necessary to be taken in the present state of affairs; and at a meeting the following day the board adopted the recommendation of the conference to decline underwriting any marine risk, peace risks excepted, "conditioned that it be adopted by the other Insurers in Philadelphia." But this action was repealed on 12 September, as the recommendation had not been carried into execution at the other offices. On 8 October another committee was raised to "wait on the Secretary of State to obtain such further information as he can furnish" on the order given by France to capture neutral vessels in order to distress the commerce of Great Britain, tidings of which had reached them "through the Newspapers and in private letters from England." On 20 January, 1797, a committee was appointed to form some rules for the Rates of Premiums in view of "the late alarming intelligence concerning Captors and Seizures of American Vessels by French Cruizers."

On 19 June, 1798, it was "agreed not to insure to French ports unless with a warranty against capture and seizure by the French."

The United States sought in various ways redress from the French government for these spoliations by the latter upon the commerce of its people; but the French held the United States to the stipulation of the treaty of 1778, in its eleventh article, that the latter should guaranty to the former forever, against all other powers, its then possessions in America. This the United States could not now do without certain collision with Great Britain, and this the country was not in a condition to encounter. France claimed that the United States had proved faithless herein, and pressed the claim against any redress for the spoliations. The United States had in various ways sought release from this guaranty, even offering a money equivalent for it, but France would not forego the letter of the article. Finally, agreement was reached by the convention of 30 September, 1800, the result of which was the two nations renounced their mutual pretensions, our government surrendering the claims of her citizens in consideration of being released by France from her guaranty. "Thus did our government, after long years of negotiation and angry contention on behalf of the claimants, after having instructed its ministers strenuously to insist upon indemnity for their wrongs, and after having secured every acknowledgment of its justice from the nation by whom it was due—by one act overthrow the whole train which was in operation for their relief— negotiate away their interests to secure public benefit, and leave them helpless and defenceless."

The claimants became alarmed at this turn of affairs and promptly took steps looking to the United States for redress. On 12 February, 1801, the directors "ordered that an account of all illegal Captures made by the British and French be made out for the purpose of representing the same to the Government of the United States, and that the President, if he should find it necessary, be empowered to employ a person for that purpose." On 6 March scales of rates were adopted to meet these piratical hazards, as such in fact they were, for the convention of September, 1800, only referred to past and brought no exemption from future spoliations; after an effort to agree upon some uniform action with the other local underwriters had failed, the only point of agreement between them being "that the risque of seizure in Port ought not to be borne by the Assurers." On 26 May a committee reported to the board that "the number and amount of the Companies' claims on the British Government for Spoliations on Property which they think that nation ought to refund is about $981,355; other losses occasioned to this office by Capture of the British and for which there is no expectation of reimbursement is about $78,800. With respect to the Captures made by the French, your Committee can only state that they amount to about $1,952,730, and that they deem it much the Interest of the Company to have them correctly arranged with all their Proofs as soon as possible, in order to demand restitution when such restitution may be expected." On 14 December, 1802, the president reports his correspondence with Mr. Hollins, president of the Maryland Insurance Company, relating to the employment of "able Counsel to

write in support of the claim which the sufferers by French
spoliations have upon the Government of the United States
in consequence of the late Treaty with France which pro-
hibits them from claiming from the French Government."
On 21 May following, the president was authorized to
confer with the presidents of other insurance companies, as
well as with private claimants, to take order respecting
applications to Congress on account of the spoliations.

But it is not needed to recite the various minutes of the
board in this grievance against the National government,
nor the various steps taken by counsel and in memorial, to
seek redress from year to year, and how twice on the eve
of success, a presidential veto, on baseless arguments, had
thrown the claimants back. Between the years 1827 and
1846, twenty-two reports of committees, all in favor of the
claimants had been made in the two houses of Congress,
each by a bill, and for five millions dollars indemnity. In
the first session of the Congress of 1846, both houses
united on a bill, which was vetoed by President Polk on
10 August, then on the eve of his war with Mexico. The
claimants, however, returned to the matter in the following
session, and in January, 1855, both houses united on the
bill, which was in its turn vetoed by President Pierce on
17 February. Each of the following Congresses witnessed
the introduction of measures of restoration, but the war of
1861 to 1865 prevented further consideration of the matter,
until in the XLVII Congress a bill was introduced by
Senator Hoar, providing for a reference of these to the
Court of Claims, which passed 15 December, 1882, but did
not reach consideration in the House. In the following

Congress the same bill was presented by Senator Frye and
passed the Senate, and reaching its passage in the House
14 January, 1885, it met the approval of President Arthur.
The Directors can now look forward to a period when the
corporation can secure some restitution for the heavy losses
of its early years.

The claims for losses by British cruisers were met under
Mr. Jay's treaty, which was ratified in 1796, by which that
government "paid to the merchants of the United States for
captured vessels an indemnity amounting to $11,650,000."
The losses by Spanish cruisers, and those for which Spain
was responsible in harboring the prizes taken by the
French, were eventually settled by the treaty which secured
to us the possession of Florida; and the directors in July,
1824, were enabled from this payment to make a dividend
of sixty per cent. to their stockholders; dividing $300,000,
when their surplus did not exceed $20,000.

The marine business of the Company exhibited some
remarkable fluctuations; and as the directors of those early
days had not learned the lesson of a solid surplus, they
divided the profits to the stockholders, not forecasting the
storms which would come, and their want of thought in
this respect, more than once brought the corporation to the
brink of ruin. The marine premiums written to the close
of the year 1793 amounted to $213,465.31, and the losses
paid, to $38,484.16. In 1794 the premiums were $290,656.83,
and they increased to $1,304,208.91 in 1798, when they began
to decrease, and in 1802 they were but $103,902.26. This
first decade showed premiums written $6,037,456.71, and
losses paid, $5,500,887.57. The premiums of 1802 were

trebled by 1805, and again in 1806; but in 1808 the premiums were but $5,843.55, and the losses, $108,568.93; and the years 1809 to 1812 inclusive, showed an annual average of but $45,449. This second decade gave premiums $1,364,637.48, and losses paid, $1,583,836.47. It will be seen farther on how different were the results during the same periods of the fire business, though in magnitude of premiums it seemed but a modest department of the company. From 1813 to 1822 inclusive, the third decade, the premiums written were but $276,764.30, while the losses paid were $335,554.06. The succeeding decade, 1823 to 1832 was yet more discouraging, for the premiums were $160,138.70, and losses $227,954.57. The years 1833 to 1842 noted the upward tendency, the premiums being $428,584.16, and the losses only $358,332.78. The decade succeeding, gave the premium account, $2,855,189.98, and the losses, $2,153,679.96.

The company began its operations at a period in the commerce of Philadelphia when its supremacy was acknowledged, and when its capitalists and shippers had their ventures in all quarters of the globe. This sceptre gradually passed from Philadelphia to its older neighbor New York, and with the enlarging number of companies at home and in other cities, and a reduction of rates, the lessening business of the company can be explained. Of their active associates in the business in the city during the first third of a century of their existence, the Phœnix (1803), Philadelphia (1804), Delaware (1804), Marine (1809), United States (1810) and Atlantic (1825), each in its time closed its business, evidencing the severe trials which marine underwriting in particular underwent at that period; and the State of Pennsylvania and the Union (1804) alone survive to testify to the struggles of those days. Of the New York companies who were contemporary with these, the Knickerbocker, as the successor of the old Mutual Assurance Company (1787) and the Eagle (1806) alone survive, and the remainder, namely, the New York (1796), Associated Underwriters (1797), United (1797), Columbian (1801), Washington Mutual (1802), Marine (1802), Commercial (1804), Phœnix (1807), Firemen's (1810), Ocean (1810), have all passed away. The oldest company in New York issuing marine policies is the Sun Mutual, organized in 1841. The oldest company in Boston so writing is the American, organized in 1818.

VI.

FIRE BUSINESS.

IMMEDIATELY after incorporation, Fire Insurance suggested itself to the directors. The two local mutual companies insured buildings alone; and no instrumentality existed to offer indemnity to merchants and manufacturers for their losses by fire on land; if the company could take all the risks of the sea, with fire included, why should it not take the risk of fire on land; and while protecting the merchant by their policies on his sea ventures, could they not offer him a policy to cover his ventures when safely landed and stored in his warehouses. At a meeting of the directors on 28 April, 1794, it was "proposed to form a Plan for Insuring Goods, Wares, and Merchandises in Dwelling Houses, Warehouses or Stores and upon Buildings, against the Risque arising from Fire"; and Messrs. Swanwick, Blodget and Fry were appointed a committee to consider the subject. The committee reported in favor of the plan on 11 July, and "on the question, will the Company insure the full sum the Goods in Store are valued at, or two-thirds of said Value, it was determined in favor of insuring the full sum, by eleven votes against one." But the summer, with its renewed visitation of yellow fever, prevented action. On 13 October, the "Proposals for Insurance," or conditions as we now style them, were adopted and ordered printed and advertised, and the new fire policy was approved on

10 November. On 24 November, William Garrigues was appointed Surveyor of Houses, and on 8 December, a badge was adopted to be attached to houses upon which policies were to be issued, agreeably to the custom of the two older mutual companies of the city, which was a wavy star of six points, cast in lead, and mounted on a wooden shield; and at the same meeting it was determined not to make any insurance on frame Houses or Stores, or on Goods in either of them; this rule was not adhered to, however, as by the minutes of 27 March, 1798, reference is made to the practice of insuring wooden buildings, and the question raised how far it will be proper to continue it. On 10 December, 1794, the first two policies were issued, namely:

No. 1. William Beynroth, on German Dry Goods, in the House No. 21 High Street, for three years, for $8,000, at 30 cents per annum, the premium being $64, which was on the scale of two and two-thirds years' premium for a term of three years.

No. 2. Lawrence Harbert, on Dry Goods, $5,000, and on Furniture and Wearing Apparel, $1,300, in the House No. 161, on the North Side of High Street, for one year, at 30 cents.

The demand for the fire policies was limited, but the amounts sometimes written on a single policy made a fair average of business.

On the 22 December, No. 6 was issued to John White-sides for $25,000, being $23,000 on Linen, Woolen and Silk Goods, and $2,000 on Furniture and Wearing Apparel, "in the Dwelling House and Store adjoining, both included in No. 136, on the South Side of High Street," for one year

1794
Policy No 1
Decem 10
B26
R

Insurance against Fire for
William Beynroth, on German Dry Goods
in House No 211 High Street, for
three Years. —

Drs 8000 at 30 Cents ⅌ ann. 72
"abate 8   64 —
Badge & Policy . . . 2 —   66
Received Cash for the above. —

Policy 2
Decr 10
B26
R
A.

prime
Renewed
Decr 8. 1795

Lawrence Herbert, on Sundries
in House No 161, on the North
Side of High Street. — Viz
for one Year
Dry Goods . . . . . Drs 5000
Household Furniture (includ-
ing a looking Glass. Valued
at Thirty five Dollars) and
Linen 500
Wearing Apparel 400
Silver plate 300
China & Glass 100
                Drs 6300
at 30 Cents . . . . Drs 18. 90
Badge & Policy . . 2   20. 90
Received Cash for the above. —

Policy 3
Decr 13
B26
R

Rundle & Murgatroyd, on
Dry Goods, in House No
on the North side of Walnut Street
for one Year — —
Dolls 8000 at 30 cts . . . . 24 —
Badge & Policy . 2 —   26

at 60 cts. No. 7 was issued on the 31st to Wells and Morris, on Ironmongery, Saddlery and Hardware, in the House No. 135 High Street, for $16,000, at 45 cts.

On 19 January, 1795, the Secretary was directed to have printed 5,000 of the "Proposals," to be distributed at the houses of the Inhabitants of the City, a stroke of activity not common in corporate circles of that day.

The badge of a star was shortly disused, for we find on 26 December, 1796, the adoption of an eagle rising from a rock, as an alternate with the star, "the Insured to have their option of the Badges"; the eagle we yet see on some of the buildings in the eastern part of the city. But one of the star badges is known to exist, and that was recognized only six years ago on the building now No. 229 south Front street, in which, upon examination of the policy register, it was found that Policy No. 4 covered $8,000 on wines and teas, for one year, at 30 cents.

The insurances at first were exclusively on town risks; but after a consideration of an extension of this branch, it was agreed on 9 March, 1795, "that Brick or Stone Houses within ten miles of the City (in Pennsylvania), may be insured against fire." A year elapsed, when greater extension was given, and 18 April, 1796, the Directors "having considered the expediency of affording the Public an opportunity to make Assurance on Buildings" from Fire beyond the limits heretofore prescribed, they determine to "allow the same, provided they be situated within the United States, and premiums adequate to the risk in the opinion of the President and Committee of the Week be paid for the same. And provided also, however, that on hazardous in

the vicinity of Philadelphia, and denominated of the first
class, no single risk shall exceed Six Thousand Dollars
unless situated in a principal Town or City, nor be accepted
at a less premium than a half ℔ cent. per annum; and provided also, that on hazards of the second class, no greater
risk on a single building shall be taken than four thousand
Dollars, and that no less a premium than three-fourths
℔ cent. annually." And "That the Insurance on Wooden
Buildings shall not be considered to be precluded by any
article in our printed proposals, but that when two or more
wooden buildings adjoin, a larger premium shall be required
than is demanded on a single wooden building." Prior to
this the same risks beyond the line sanctioned 9 March,
1795, had been accepted, and on 29 February, it was
resolved, "the Insurances which have been so made be and
they are hereby approved and confirmed." On 27 February,
1798, "the Board is of opinion that it is not expedient to
have an Agent at Charleston authorised to take Risques
against Fire," which minute points to the first offers of a
distant agency. On 19 April, 1798, a total loss on a risk on
Maiden lane, New York, was suspected to be of incendiary
origin, and a reward of $1,000 was offered "for discovering
and prosecuting" the supposed incendiary, which was duly
advertised in the New York papers.

On 16 January, 1804, the president referred to the board
"the demands of applicants for insurances against fire to
have the premiums reduced" which the board were not
prepared to order, leaving them to the president and the
committees to make according as they should deem it
expedient where circumstances would fairly admit of small

INSURANCE

AGAINST LOSS OR DAMAGE BY FIRE

BY THE

Insurance Company of North America.

THE President and Directors of the Insurance Company of North America, in the City of Philadelphia, being desirous to employ the capital of said company to purposes useful to the public as well as beneficial to the institution, have resolved to extend their Insurances against losses or damage by Fire, to the various parts of the United States, on buildings of every description, as well as on goods, wares, and merchandise of all kinds. And upon such moderate and liberal terms, as it is presumed will induce every to avail themselves of the means thus offered, to protect themselves from the destructive injury so frequently occasioned by fire.

Among the various claims which have been made against the company for losses by fire since its first establishment (now more than thirteen years) no instance of a legal controversy has occurred to the terms the company and the assured. But on the contrary, all claims for losses of this nature, have been adjusted and paid with that utmost promptitude, which circumstances, together with the ample capital the company possess, gives them a fair claim to public confidence.

RATES OF ANNUAL PREMIUMS TO BE PAID FOR ASSURANCES AGAINST FIRE.

No. I. Hazards of the First Class, &c.	No. II. Hazards of the Second Class, &c.	No. III. Hazards of the Third Class, &c.	No. IV. Hazards of the Fourth Class, &c.

CONDITIONS OF INSURANCE.

I. Persons desirous to make insurance in building in places where the Company have no agent, must accompany their applications with a description of the property to be assured, to be made by a master carpenter, and signed by him as well as by the owner or applicant...

V. No Insurance will be effected on any wooden building, or on property therein, to an amount exceeding two thirds the value thereof.

JOHN INSKEEP, *President.*

---

alterations, "so, however, as not to go below 25 cents for $100 per annum." This doubtless may have been induced by the increased competition of the two new companies, the Union and the Phœnix, who as well added fire underwriting to marine, and who began operations before incorporation was consummated.

On 19 May, 1807 the society for protecting property from loss in case of fire made application for assistance, and the president was directed "to pay as a Contribution to said Company the sum of $50." This institution was the early forerunner of our present Fire Patrol, but of its work and its duration we find here no further trace.

Policies had been from time to time issued covering properties in distant localities where the applicant had been known to the company; this led to extending the business more systematically; and on 6 October, 1807 Mr. Alexander Henry presented an address "on the subject of extending Insurances against Fire to Lexington, in Kentucky," on which Messrs. Henry, Taylor and Read "were appointed a Committee to consider as to the benefit and propriety of extending insurances against Fire generally to other Cities and Towns in other States beyond what is now customary to take." On 3 November the committee's favorable report was adopted, and they were directed "to digest and report such limitations, regulations and restrictions as it may be thought prudent to recommend." And on 1 December, the board adopted their resolutions, which were carefully drawn, looking to a cautious business, one of which empowered the president "to appoint suitable and trusty persons at such places as he shall think advisable to act as

Surveyors and Agents of the Company," and "to instruct
each agent of the Company as to the execution of his trust
and furnish him with such information as he may think
proper." This was the beginning of a fire agency business
which half a century developed into such great and profitable proportions. From a little manuscript book entitled
"Fire Agents," in President Inskeep's handwriting, recently
found in the files of the company, we obtain some particulars of this agency work which are worthy of record here.
By this we learn on 22 January, 1808, Charles Ellis was
appointed agent at Burlington, James Ewing at Trenton;
on the 23d, Andrew Ross at Washington; on the 26th,
Ephraim Holmes at Bridgeton; and at "Towns Westward,"
Jesse Hunt at Cincinnati, Peter Lee at Washington, Thomas
McCall at Lexington, Jeptha Dudley at Frankfort, John
Bustard at Louisville, Thomas Howard at Richmond. On
3 February, among others, Jacob Hay at York Town,
John Creigh at Carlisle, Edward Crawford at Chambers-
burg, Robert Brown at Greensburg, James M. Caldwell
at Wheeling, John McCoy at Chillicothe, Doctor John
McDowell at Steubenville, William Tate at Nashville, and
on 6 February, Robert Boggs at New Brunswick. Mr.
Dudley held the agency at Frankfort for thirty years, his
resignation being noticed at the directors' meeting of 8
January, 1838. On 20 February, Mr. Inskeep wrote to
Marks John Biddle, Esq., of Reading, "I take the liberty
to send you some of our Proposals, form of a survey, and
letter of appointment for an agent, which I will thank you
to direct to some suitable person in your place who will act
as such for this Company. I should be pleased if you

would accept the agency yourself, but this I can scarcely hope, as the magnitude of your own concerns will probably forbid it." Mr. Biddle selected and appointed Mr. Frederick Fritz, and this was the beginning of an agency which to this day has been continuously filled with faithful and competent representatives. *

This extension of the company's business found a motive in the establishment by the Phœnix Insurance Company of London of agencies in this country; and as their experiment had been successful, the time had arrived for the North America to secure the like footing at distant places. But the Phœnix may have resorted to flexible rates when this home company entered the agency field, if we can so conclude from a letter Mr. Inskeep wrote 14 March, 1808 to

---

* The following is the first letter of the president to the new agent, and displays the caution with which the "agency business" was conducted. "29 March, 1808. I am pleased to hear from Marks John Biddle, Esquire, that you have accepted the agency of the Company for the Borough of Reading. I have received your survey of Mr. George Keim's property, which is very minute and circumstantial. The risque would have been a very good one was it not for the circumstance of the Oil and Paints being kept in the cellar, and the Tavern being so nearly situated. I will, however, agree to take the Risque at 40 cts. per $100, for one year—should the premium be agreeable, the amount as per statement at foot may be remitted, and on the receipt of which the Insurance will be binding. The policies shall be forwarded by Post or otherwise as may be directed." These were numbered 5,003 for $1,000, "on a Stone House or Building, Kitchen and Store adjoining and belonging thereto, Situate on the north side of Penn Street, in the Centre Square, near the Court House, in the Borough of Reading," and No. 5,004, for $5,000, "on Goods or Merchandize contained in the one and an half Story Store adjoining the assured's Dwelling," all at 40 cts. for one year. Both had the following endorsement: "Notwithstanding the foregoing restriction, It is agreed that the assured shall have permission to store in the above named Store, *Gunpowder, Spirit of Turpentine*, and *Oil*, together with such other articles in small quantities as are usually kept in a retail Country Store." Charge was made for a badge of $2, and for two policies, $2. The only remuneration to the agent being his survey fee from the assured.

Mr. Ewing at Trenton, viz : "I am aware that the Phœnix Insurance Company of London do take risks both in and out of this City at a lower premium than we do in this office, and that without much investigation. We find, however, that a decided preference is given to our office at higher premiums than they generally ask, the reasons for which, people must judge for themselves—it does not belong to me to assign them." The Phœnix came here in 1806, but withdrew its agencies in a few years, but re-entered the United States in 1879. One of its original "Proposals" issued in Philadelphia, was found in 1880 among the papers of the North America, where it yet remains. In 1807 the Pelican Insurance Company of London was represented in New York, but it was without any representative in Philadelphia.

The expiration of fire polices was notified to policy-holders by advertisement in the daily papers, in monthly lists; whether the assured was a citizen of Philadelphia or of Charleston, his reminder was obtained only through the Philadelphia papers. The general results of the fire business were satisfactory to the directors, but it was in these early years looked upon only as an adjunct to their marine business in its convenience to their customers; and Mr. Stephens, the secretary, often referred in his semi-annual reports to the profits of this business as meeting the expenses of the office, showing that it was relied upon to defray the current expense of the office, which it more than did, so that the marine business in its fluctuations and uncertainties should not be exposed to the charge of office support. Secretary Stephens in his report to the stock-

ON GOODS. (For *Twelve* Months.)

BY THE PRESIDENT AND DIRECTORS OF THE INSURANCE COMPANY OF NORTH AMERICA.

No. 5453   WHEREAS, *John Ashley*

hath paid to the President and Directors of the Insurance Company of North America Thirty-five dollars for the Insurance of Eight thousand dollars on his Household and Kitchen Furniture comprehending among articles, wrought silver, plate, china, and glass, and on wearing apparel, linen, printed books, prints and maps, not more valued at one thousand and thirty dollars contained in his three story brick dwelling House & Kitchen situated on the West side of Fourth between Walnut and Prune street, in this City of Philada.

EARLY FIRE POLICY ON GOODS, 1809.

holders January, 1825, says: "the fire business meets expenses as it ordinarily does when no losses occur." The extension of the business to other localities was to increase this profitable result, and at a time when marine insurance in this country was disastrous and had a very doubtful future. We might suppose that had in the outstart more direct attention been paid to this branch, larger returns would have been had and the company have been proportionably benefited; but we must recollect that fire insurance was in its infancy comparatively, and the insurer in a community, was the exception, and not the rule. The large lines written by the company were evidence of the want of proper knowledge of the danger in so writing, but it was on the other hand evidence that the moral hazard was more certain, as the danger from frequent fires was lessened by the fact that the major portion of any community was entirely uninsured, and the want of a guarantee of indemnity in case of loss, perforce made this class of people more heedful to the dangers of fire and watchful of their interests. To the close of the year 1802, embracing eight years and twenty days, the fire premiums received amounted to $81,253.76, and the losses, which first began in 1797, $30,116.59. The next ten years were better—premiums, $98,647.95; losses, $23,873.30; the succeeding decade was remarkable in its figures—premiums, $69,224.20; losses, $1,569.44, the years 1814, 1816–19 and 1822, not showing a dollar of loss on a premium receipt of $42,380.79. From 1823 to 1832, premiums were $61,639.33; losses, $17,973; the decade following, premiums, $114,326.34; losses, $78,948.27. From 1843 to 1852, premiums, $354,267.08;

losses, $382,407.43; this last period embraced the losses by
the great fire in the vicinity of Vine and Callowhill, westward from the wharves, July, 1850, after which there was
an acknowledgment of the inadequacy of fire premiums in
Philadelphia on the part of the companies, which led to
action in October following, which would have been united
and common but for one company declining to agree to
advanced rating. The years 1843 to 1852 mark the development of the modern system of an agency business,
for the receipts had quintupled those of the preceding
ten years. The decade following showed a larger business and with better results; premiums, $1,138,164.24;
losses, $424,448.32. The next decade showed a premium
receipt of eight times the amount of its predecessor; and
the premiums for the year 1884 alone exceeded the com-
bined premium receipts of the first sixty-eight years of the
Company's operations; the average loss in this long period
being but 45.3 per cent. of the premiums.

On 28 January, 1840, a committee was appointed to prepare a form of perpetual policy, the recent supplement to
the charter enabling the company to enter on this business,
but the final steps were deferred, and authority was only
formally given to the officers on 4 May, 1841, and the first
policy was shortly thereafter issued; and to the close of the
year 1846 a loss of but $62.09 was made upon a net deposit
receipt of $5,781.55. To the close of the year 1872, the
losses had been but twelve and one-half per cent. of the net
deposit receipts; but a proper mode to calculate the perpetual business is to base the losses upon the interest of the
net balances, and the result in this instance will show the

losses of the company to be about one-third of the interest account on their perpetual deposit balances, and after adding its proper expenses, leaving the deposit untouched, (subject to call as it may be,) and a profit beside.

The beginnings of the fire business, modest in the extreme, have grown in our day to a figure which the first board of directors never contemplated, any more than they could contemplate the immense growth of the nation in its wealth and population. The wealth of those days was to be found on the Atlantic board, and shipping was the most familiar and perhaps the most respectable calling, and opened the most promising avenue to the rising generations for the extension of their activities. But wars and the changes in the courses of trade made the uncertainties of sea ventures more conspicuous, while the silent but sure growth of inland interests was outstepping them in attraction, until in our day we find the best energies of our people given to internal development, and for the success of this corporate underwriting must and will be had, and the future of fire underwriting seems illimitable so long as we cannot measure or bound our national growth. And we must admit that marine underwriting, even with its peculiar fascinations, has lost its rank of prominence, and that fire underwriting is now and will remain in the forefront.

VII.

LIFE BUSINESS.

THE first action had under the clause of the articles of association permitting Life Insurance was on 20 January, 1794, when Messrs. Fitzsimons, Ball and McMurtrie were appointed "a Committee to consider of a Policy for insuring persons against Capture by Algerines, etc." This was at once formulated, for on 11 February following, they insured Captain John Collet, "on his Person against Algerines and other Barbary Corsairs in a Voyage from Philadelphia to London, in the Ship *George Barclay*, himself Master, Valuing himself at $5,000," the premium on which was two per cent. On 7 March, Captain Samuel Hubbell, of the ship *Eagle*, bound from Baltimore to Oporto or Lisbon, was insured in like manner for $4,000 at five per cent. On 13 May following, Thomas Baker, master of the brig *Hector* at and from Bordeaux to Philadelphia for $4,000, the premium of which was five per cent. These insurances were "declared to be made upon the person of * * * against the risque of Capture by the Algerines or any of the Barbary Corsairs only, and it is mutually agreed between the Parties to this Policy, that if the said * * * should be killed in any attempts made to defend the said Brig against the said Algerines or Corsairs, or should die before or after his Captivity and before he should be Ransomed, the Assurers shall not be bound to pay any other Sum or Sums than what may have been expended in attempting the Ransom of the said * *

It was not until 9 January, 1795, that it was decided to undertake some plan for insurances on lives, and Messrs. Blodget, Fry and Breck were appointed a committee to form a plan, and the same must have been put into use by the officers without reference to the board, although the individual applications for life policies were in each instance passed upon by the board. But the demand was light, for not until 24 May, 1796, do we find the approval of the first two life insurances, viz., on the life of John Holker from 6 June to 19 September inclusive, for $24,000 at one and a half per cent., which, however, appears not to have been accepted; and "on the natural life of Bon Albert Briois de Beaumez (who attained the age of Forty-one years in the month of December now last past, and is about to sail for India * *), for and during the term and space of Eighteen Calendar months" for $5,000. A guaranty in this policy as to continuance of the life of the subject is made in the following phrase: "The said President and Directors, therefore and in consideration of Ten per cent. to them paid, do assure, assume and promise that he the said Bon Albert Briois de Beaumez shall, by the permission of Almighty God, live and continue in this natural Life for and during said Term and space of Eighteen Calendar months * *." On the 27 September following, $8,000 was agreed to be insured on the life of Colonel Tousard for one year at eight per cent., "with permission for him to go and remain in the West Indies during that Period"; but the policy seems not to have been issued.

On 15 February, 1803, an insurance for ten thousand dollars
was agreed to "on the Life of General de Noailles (who is
now supposed to be in the Havana) for six months at the
rate of five per cent., he being prohibited from acting as an
officer or soldier in any military expedition, or from returning to the West Indies after his arrival here during the
continuance of the said Risque." And the last we find
agreed to was on 9 April, 1804, on the life of Mr. George
Meade: but neither of these policies were issued. The
premiums named by the company on the life applications
may have prevented in many cases acceptance of its policies,
as is shown in the cases now cited. Mr. Hazard in respond-
ing 20 November, 1799 to the inquiries of Mr. Henry
Remsen, made on behalf of the Manhattan Company of
New York, as to the mode of conducting the insurance
business in its different branches, stated regarding the life
branch: "There have been but few instances of this kind,
perhaps half a dozen, in each of which we have gained the
premium. Price's tables are those we have used, as far as
tables have been recurred to." This branch of the business
seemed not to have survived a decade, nor was the company
induced afterwards to renew or cultivate it, and not until
the incorporation of the Pennsylvania Company for Insurances on Lives and Granting Annuities in 1812 was it that
the subject of life insurance secured any development and
extension in this community.

VIII.

FINANCES.

THE statement of premiums given on previous pages indicate that the finances of the company underwent many and severe fluctuations. Success early favored the projectors, and divisions of profits were promptly realized to the advantage of the stockholder personally, but to the detriment of the corporation. The dividends paid from July, 1793, to January, 1798, inclusive, amounted to $591,296.63; but in July following the balance of the company's accounts was on the debtor side. In January, 1799, a dividend of twenty per cent. was made, viz.: $120,000, followed in the next semi-annual period by a heavy balance again on the debtor side. This condition of the company continued up to January, 1807, when a dividend of four per cent. was made, and the company by this time was owner of 3,770 of its own shares. Dividends continued with some degree of regularity to 1812, inclusive. Three years followed without any profits to divide. In July, 1816, the company owned 7,534 of its shares; by July, 1835, it became possessed of 13,959 shares, purchasing to save them from the market; and the assets, including these, amounted to $683,021.50. The highest assets prior to this were in January, 1809, when they amounted to $722,699.03. In 1842 an equalization was had of their condition, by a reduction of the capital, alluded to before, to five dollars a share,

and the assets were on 1 January, 1843, $385,060.92,
including 13,459 shares. On 1 January, 1850, the assets
had increased to $911,667.40, and the company only own-
ing 12,000 shares. By 1 January, 1853, the assets were
$964,681,49, the company having parted with all its shares
formerly held by it, but the capital had been increased in
1851 to $500,000. On 1 January, 1858, the assets were
$1,007,825.26. Ten years later the assets had reached
$1,962,836.54, while dividends amounting to $900,000 had
been paid in the same time. In 1874 the capital stock was
doubled, and this in 1876 was in its turn doubled, making
it now two million dollars. The decade ending 1 January,
1878, showed rapid but substantial progress, the assets on
that date being $6,408,696.58, the dividends paid during
the same period (excepting 1873 when dividends were
passed, due to the Boston losses of November, 1872)
amounting to $1,170,000, while the surplus had increased
from $237,753.36 to $2,362,532.34. In 1881 the happy con-
summation of a joint increase of the capital and surplus
was effected by increasing the stock to three million dollars,
and apportioning the one hundred thousand new shares to
the stockholders at the rate of twenty dollars per share,
being double the par. On 1 January, 1885, the assets
amounted to $9,079,481.40, showing an increase in seven-
teen years of $7,116,644.66, from which when is deducted
the new capital paid up $2,500,000, and the cash increase
of $1,000,000 in the surplus, we find that in this period the
gain from its business and investments alone amounted to
the sum of $3,616,644.66.

The Assurance Company of North America.

To Thomas Mackie Dr.

1793
Feby 2d. To Rent of your offices known as Bennett's offices
per act. at the rate of £200 per
annum at the rate of £200 — Dollars 114 43/100

Received payment &c. Feby 11 1793

Thos Markoe

IX.

OFFICE LOCATIONS.

IT may be interesting to follow the company through its various offices, and call up pictures of the localities in which it found itself from time to time. It steadily maintained itself nigh to the haunts of the city's business, and we shall thus be able to obtain glimpses of some of its neighbors and associates and some studies of that section of the city in which centered Philadelphia's mercantile wealth.

It is elsewhere stated that the new board met at six o'clock, P. M., on 14 December, 1792, in their own offices, which were in the brick building No. 119 (now 213) south Front street. This building remains substantially unchanged to this day, and is one of the few original edifices left in the block. A very faithful etching of it was made in the spring of 1880 by Mr. Pennell, a member of the Philadelphia Etching Club. Nearly opposite, at No. 96 (now 212), lived Mr. Nesbitt, the president, the counting-house of his firm, Conyngham, Nesbitt & Co., being on the first floor; next door, No. 117, lived Mr. Jasper Moylan, a director, and later their counsel; at No. 115, Messrs. Isaac Wharton and David Lewis, merchants and insurance brokers, had their office; and immediately south of No. 119 was the large building owned by Mr. John Ross, a director, occupied by the custom-house. On the

opposite side of Front street there dwelt at the time, besides
Mr. Nesbitt, Robert Ralston at No. 90, Miers Fisher, No.
92, Peter Blight, No. 102, Nalbro Frazier. No. 104, Francis
West, No. 108, Samuel R. Fisher, No. 110, Mordecai Lewis,
No. 112, and John Morton at No. 116. Shortly after their
settlement in these offices, proposals were made to the board
by the trustees for the Philadelphia Dancing Assembly to
unite in erecting a suitable building for their joint uses;
the proposals were submitted * to Mr. Nesbitt and Col.
Pettit, but no further reference appears on the minutes to
the subject.

Here the company continued until February, 1794, the
only intermission to their business being caused by the
ravages of yellow fever in 1793, which was particularly
severe in that quarter of the city. Mr. Nesbitt left the city
in September and passed the remainder of the season at
Clermont, the residence of his partner, Mr. David H.
Conyngham, a handsome property with a fine mansion,
situate at the southeasterly junction of Nicetown lane and
Hart lane, a place afterwards known as Mrs. Griscom's
famous school.

Mr. Nesbitt, who was not in robust health, had probably
been passing his nights out of the city previously, for on
24 September, 1793, he writes to Mr. Hazard, "I went to
Town on Monday to see what was to do, but found things in
our Neighbourhood in such a Situation I thought it Improper

---

* The Dancing Assembly proposed that each should advance £6,000; the lot
to belong to the Insurance Company, joint agents or trustees to be appointed
for the management of the business, letting the house, &c., and the money
arising from rent, &c., to be divided between the Insurance Company and the
Dancing Assembly.

to remain. Indeed I should have long since quit our own business, for that was arranged so as to make my presence unnecessary, but I did not like to decline my place in the Insurance office while I could remain in Town with any degree of personal safety, and if any applications are made, I shall, if sent out to me here, attend to and answer them as I do my own business." Mr. Hazard had written him on the 23d: "The situation of our Neighbourhood I find has become truly alarming; in going to and returning from it, I am much exposed to Infection, and it does not appear necessary to attend longer at the Office, as so little Business offers; were there more, it could not be done, as I am now quite alone. Mr. Coulthard [the clerk who had been appointed 18 December, 1792] went a few miles into the country on Saturday afternoon and intended returning this morning; but as it is now one o'clock, and I have not yet seen him, I fear he is sick; there are no Directors whom I can consult on this Occasion: thus Situated, I have concluded to remove the Books and Papers, for the present, to my own house, where I shall be constantly ready to attend to anything that offers."

Thus exposed, and without clerical help, Mr. Hazard moved the office work to his house, No. 145 Arch street, on the site of which is erected the easternmost of Mr. Womrath's improvement, and is now No. 415. Mr. Hazard built this house in 1792, and there he resided until his death in 1817, when his heirs sold it, Mr. William Sansom (who was a director in the company 1795–97) purchasing it for his daughter, Mrs. George Vaux, whose family occupied it until they sold it to Mr. Womrath, who also purchased the adjoining property on the west, for many years owned and occupied by Mr. John Cooke.

Mr. Hazard and eight others of his household succumbed to the epidemic, two of whom died from it; and here he remained until 9 November, when the approach of cool weather rendered it safe to return to the office to Front street, and clients would feel no hesitation in going thither. He had communicated daily with Mr. Nesbitt, but from 28 September to 11 October, his letters ceased, showing the time and duration of his illness. He had here himself written fifty-three policies, whose premiums amounted to $16,875.32, and kept up the books and all the correspondence of the company. The faithful porter, John Valentine Cline, always called Valentine, and recorded on the company's books as Doorkeeper, rode out daily on horseback to Clermont and exchanged letters with Mr. Nesbitt. This correspondence is preserved entire, and each letter is duly endorsed by the receiver; and thus we have in the company's files a complete picture of the terrors of that awful visitation, whose mortality amounted to one in four of the population which continued in the city, the deaths in all amounting to five thousand in those few dreadful weeks. All Mr. Hazard's letters and enclosures coming from his fever-stricken house were passed through disinfectants at Clermont before being there read, and the papers show marks of the treatment to this day. But the enclosures were often returned by Mr. Nesbitt, the worse for such, and on 22 October, Mr. Hazard writes him: "If a less quantity of *vinegar* will answer the purpose, perhaps it will be best not to put so much on the Papers, as it defaces them; I do not know whether it will destroy the writing. but if it will, it may be very injurious in case of a Law suit or Reference in which these Papers must be produced."

In February, 1794, the company rented the premises No. 107 south Front street, at the southeast corner of Walnut street, at £100 and taxes per annum, and there moved 1 March. It was on the 10 December following, the first fire policy of the company was here issued. They subleased to Mr. Alexander Todd "that part of the House of Company's office now occupied by him, for £25 per annum." This building was destroyed some years ago, and the present warehouse erected on its site. Within a twelvemonth, the directors felt their business warranted the purchase of a property for its transaction, and Messrs. Pettit and Ball, with the president, were appointed a committee to purchase a lot, with or without buildings. Yet another twelvemonth elapsed, however, before they could consummate their plans, and on 12 December, 1796, they purchased the premises on the opposite corner, No. 84 south Front street, at the southwest corner of Walnut, being a lot nineteen feet by eighty, with a main and back building thereon, for £3,400; but they appear not to have obtained possession until the close of the following year, for we find on 14 December, 1797, a committee (Messrs. Breck, Blight and Francis) was "appointed to view the house and consider what part of it will be wanted for the accommodation of the Office and Doorkeeper."

The occasion of this appointment was a communication from Col. Pettit, the president, "respecting accommodations in the new building." On 19 December, they "reported,

That the following apartments in the said Building are absolutely necessary for the accommodation of the Company; the large room on the ground floor; the lower room in the back building; the whole of the second story of the house, with sufficient room in the Cellar and Vault to hold their fire wood." And the directors "permitted the President of this Board, in consideration of his present indisposition, to occupy until the next election of Directors, such rooms in the new building as are not necessary for the accommodation of their office, leaving also a room for their messenger." Col. Pettit had been so indisposed for some months that at the annual meeting the following month, he declined re-election, and Mr. Joseph Ball was elected president; but Mr. Ball resigned in July, 1799, owing to pressure of private affairs, and Col. Pettit having regained his health, was re-elected, and continued in office until his death in 1806. He had kept his residence in the building, as shown by the city directories, and when the office was removed in 1804, he changed it to the corner of Second and Dock streets, where he died.

The back building had been "lately occupied by M. Moreau de St. Mery as a printing office," and this the board proposed "to rent to some Person who will not use it in any hazardous business." In the following May, Dr. James Mease became the tenant, and here his office appears to have remained until 17 June, 1800. His rent for the first year was £50; but in 1799 he claimed this "was much too high, considering the present state of affairs, and the universal diminution of the value of houses in the city, and he had no doubt they will experience a further fall," and his offer of $100 for the second year was accepted. The city directory for 1799 records Dr. Mease at No. 14 Walnut street.

In the years 1797 and 1798, other visitations of yellow fever scattered all who had business in the eastern part of the city. On 25 August, 1797, the president and secretary were "Vested with power to remove the office either to another part of the City or out of it, in case of such an increase of the present disorder as shall lead them to think it expedient." Three days later Mr. Hazard writes to Mr. Ralston "of a proposed removal of the office to Market or Arch street, between Ninth and Twelfth, but thought they might as well go to Wilmington as there"; and on the 31st advises him they have "decided to remove to Arch street, to a handsome, new, neat, airy room, with three windows, chimney piece, &c., in style." They became tenants of Mrs. Mary Kean, but the precise location cannot now be determined.

In 1798 the company's books and papers were removed to Germantown, to the old academy on School House Lane, a meeting of the directors being had there on 8 September. In the *True American* of 14 August, is an advertisement:

> "The office of the Insurance Company of North America is removed to the School-house, near the Market, in Germantown. Orders for insurance left at the South East corner of Arch and Sixth streets will be duly forwarded."

On 8 January, 1799, there is a minute, "It is left to the President and Secretary to make provision at Germantown for the accommodation of the office that there may be a certainty of a suitable Retreat in Case any Contagious

Disorder shall make it necessary to remove from the city next summer." And on the 14th, "The Board agreed to take certain rooms in Mr. Samuel Billings' house at Germantown for the next season at $300." This house is the stone dwelling, No. 4804 Germantown avenue, adjoining the Germantown National Bank building at the corner of School street, and was the building which the United States Bank occupied during the epidemic of 1793; hither Mr. Hazard moved with his family and the company's books when the "Disorder" made its appearance; the front parlor and two large rooms on the second floor were those leased. His letters thence to Col. Pettit, who had just resumed the presidency, and who had remained in the city, are yet on file, covering a period from 19 September to 7 October; there was no meeting of the board from 6 August to 4 November; Mr. Stephens, the bookkeeper, afterwards first clerk and subsequently secretary of the company from 1806 to 1832, remained also in town forwarding all applications and proposals for insurance to Germantown, as doubtless he had done the previous year, as specified in the advertisement. On 23 September, Mr. Hazard writes, "We had heard that the Fever Alarm has encreased, and are sorry to be informed if so much Cause for it as apparently well founded Reports intimate, from what we hear, the prevailing Opinion here is that the Banks will yet be removed." Mr. James Murray, the clerk, who remained with the company until 1806, had accompanied Mr. Hazard, and on 19 September, he writes, "The Dysentery has left Mr. Murray very weak, but he is convalescent. I hope Valentine won't share the Fate of his Brother Janitor." On 2 October he writes "the information that the Fever is abating, is very pleasing. * * * I hear numbers arguing that it will not be safe to return before there is a smart Frost to render City Air salubrious." The board subsequently testified their appreciation of the labors of those employed in the office during the contagion, by voting Mr. Murray $200, and Messrs. Stephens and Chas. P. Heath (the fire insurance clerk who remained with the company until 1809) $100 each, for their "services and attention," and to Valentine, the Doorkeeper, $60, for "his extraordinary services during the prevalence of the Yellow Fever." This faithful servant of the company, John Valentine Cline, remained on active duty in the office until March, 1828, when he was voted an annuity of $100, he being then, Mr. Stephens records, about eighty-two years old. Before he entered the service of the company he had been twenty years with Col. Pettit, who wrote Mr. Nesbitt, on 15 December, 1792, endorsing his application, "it is due to his merit that I should say I always found him honest, sober, diligent and attentive to his duty."

In January, 1804, a committee was "appointed to make inquiries respecting a suitable house or apartments in the neighbourhood of the Exchange," which was at the time on the west side of Second street, between Walnut street and the City Tavern, as the directors felt they were not, while in Front street, near enough to the centre of business. Failing to purchase the premises No. 98 (now 204) south Second street from Captain John McKeever, they leased the building, and by the 3d February had moved thither. Adjoining on the north, No. 96, was the Phœnix Insurance

Company, who had purchased that property the previous
year, and at No. 94, the corner of Walnut street, was the
Philadelphia Insurance Company. Captain McKeever's
house, built about 1761, by Benjamin Paschall, who in 1777
became one of the Associate Justices of the Orphans
Court of Philadelphia County, yet remains in good condition. Here the company continued for five years until they
could secure a property by purchase, which they did on 16
November, 1809, by purchasing for $12,600, Mr. William
Meredith's lot and buildings, where that eminent lawyer
had lived for some years, on the south side of Walnut
street, immediately east of Second street, extending through
to Dock street, being Nos. 40 and 42 (now 136 and 138)
Walnut street. Hither they moved in January, 1810,
renting No. 42 to the Delaware Insurance Company at the
sum of $500 per annum, on a three years' lease from 1 Feb-
ruary. The remainder of the company's lease of No. 98
south Second street was taken by Mr. John F. Watson, the
author of the *Annals of Philadelphia*, who moved his
residence and book store there on Monday, 5 February, as
recorded by Mr. Stephens in his office memorandum book.

Besides their neighbor, the Delaware Insurance Company, of which Mr. Thomas Fitzsimons, an early director
of the North America, was now president, there were nigh
the Philadelphia, Samuel W. Fisher, president, at the southwest corner of Second and Walnut streets; the State of
Pennsylvania, James S. Cox, president, at the northeast
corner of Dock and Second (adjoining the Dock street
front of the North America premises); the Phœnix, David
Lewis, president, at No. 96 (now 202) south Second street;

the Union Mutual, Joseph Ball, president, who had been president of the North America from January, 1797 to July, 1798, at No. 45 (now 129) Walnut street, opposite; the Marine and Fire, John Leamy, president, who had been a director of the North America from 1792 to 1806, at No. 49 (now 133) Walnut street; and the United States, Israel Pleasants, president, at No. 49 (now 133) Walnut street. The Philadelphia Contributionship, was at this period located at No. 99 (now 239) Market street, Caleb Carmalt, treasurer; and the Mutual Assurance Company, John B. Palmer, treasurer, was at this period without a settled habitation, and applications were received at the counting house of Mr. Palmer's partner, Mr. Robert Wharton, on Pine street wharf; its monthly meetings had been for many years held at Hardie's tavern, on the south side of Market street, and in 1809 and later at Heads' Mansion House Hotel, Third street above Spruce, until the office was finally established at No. 54 (now 226) Walnut street. It was in February of this year (1810) that was incorporated the American Fire Insurance Company, the first chartered in this State for a general fire insurance business, the Contributionship and the Mutual Assurance Company confining themselves to building insurances alone; Captain William Jones was the first president, and Mr. Edward Fox its originator, who was one of the first stockholders of the North America, the first secretary; and its office was open at No. 73 (now 229) Chestnut street, but in a few weeks was removed to the building it purchased of Mr. Moses Levy at No. 101 (now 311) Chestnut street, adjoining the bank of North America. The first advertisement of the

American commended the operations of the company to
the citizens on the grounds of its "not risking its funds by
making any Insurance on marine or other hazardous adventures, being confined by law to the sole and single object
of insuring against loss by or damage by FIRE." The
same year witnessed the creation of the African Insurance
Company, which was located at No. 159 (now 529) Lombard
street, Joseph Randolph, president, Cyrus Porter, treasurer,
William Coleman, secretary, with a cash capital of $5,000.
"The members of this Company are all colored persons,"
as stated in the directories for 1811 and 1813. In the latter
year it was located at No. 155 Lombard street, which
appears to have been the residence of its secretary, whose
profession was given as "teacher." We find no traces of it
after this year; some of its policies are yet preserved in the
families of its insured.

The Delaware Insurance Company continued to occupy
No. 42 Walnut street until the middle of the year 1814, and
was succeeded the following April as tenants by Messrs.
Pratt and Dundas until 1822, and later by Mr. Thomas
Newman, stock and exchange broker, until October, 1831.
The Dock street front had contained the office of Mr.
Nicholas Biddle, "Attorney at Law," who remained the
company's tenant until November, 1811; Mr. William
Cramond (who had been a director of the company from
its organization to 1800) occupied this office from April,
1816 to April, 1819, and was succeeded by Thomas and
John Wharton, insurance brokers. The company remained
here for a quarter of a century, with but one intermission
of a month during the prevalence of the yellow fever in the

summer of 1820, when they rented the premises No. 240 (now 710) Market street, where the office was maintained from 7 September to 7 October.

The directors desiring to keep near the centre of business, which had made another step westward, sought a location opposite the new Merchants' Exchange, then just erected, and entered into an agreement with Mr. Thomas P. Cope (a director of the company from 1829 to 1854), who owned the lot at the southwest corner of Walnut and Dock streets, to rent the westernmost office of the building he was about erecting, and on its completion they moved into it 25 August, 1834. The office was known as on Walnut street one door west of Dock street, and is now No. 216, and was taken on a lease of twenty years. The premises, now vacated by them, they sold in 1836 to Mr. John Garrison for $14,000.

But before the expiration of this lease they needed larger accommodations, and again sought quarters of their own in the immediate neighborhood. On 8 January, 1850, they purchased at public sale for $16,000, the premises then owned by the Philadelphia Exchange Company, which had purchased them in 1833, known as No. 60 (now 232) Walnut street, extending through to Pear street, being 17 feet 3 inches front by 138 feet deep; there was a four story, rough-cast building on Walnut street, occupied on the first floor by a tailor store, and on the upper floors by Messrs. Draper & Co., the well-known bank-note engravers, and on Pear street front there was a three story brick building. The front building was not adapted to the purposes of their business, and it was removed, and a new structure was erected by A. Masson, at a cost of $5,350, on plans furnished by Mr. Gervase Wheeler, an English architect, temporarily sojourning in Philadelphia, extending about 85 feet in depth, leaving a pleasant garden over 50 feet deep to Pear street, the dwelling on the end being removed. This new building was occupied 11 December, 1851; Messrs. Brown, Jones and Neff were the building committee; and at the first meeting of the board held in it, the directors "tendered their cordial thanks to them for their valuable services in planning and directing the construction of the beautifully appropriate building in which the Board convenes for the first time this morning." The balance of the company's lease from Mr. Cope for the former office was taken by Mr. Joseph Cowperthwait for his proposed new insurance company, for which a charter was procured at the next Legislature, and known as the "Philadelphia," the former of that name having some years before retired from business.

The growth of the company's affairs in the next two decades proved these accommodations inadequate, and in 1872 communication was had with the Farquhar building on the east, and two large rooms therein leased for the officers and a directors' room; and in 1874 a three story building was erected on the end of the lot adjoining the main office, and the pleasant garden was no more. But five years after this, a period which showed the greatest advance ever made in the company's business up to that time, the directors looked for yet more commodious quarters; and on 15 January, 1880, purchased for $70,000, from the estate of the late Edward Y. Farquhar, the property adjoining on the east, and known as the Farquhar Buildings, being 35

FRONT VIEW OF BUILDINGS ON SITE OF WHICH THE NORTH AMERICA'S BUILDING WAS ERECTED 1880.

feet front by 138 feet deep. This building had been erected by Mr. Farquhar in 1850, on the site of two buildings then known as Nos. 56 and 58 Walnut street, and had been occupied exclusively for offices. Within two months this building was vacated by its tenants, and plans were adopted for a suitable building to cover both the old and new premises as prepared by Messrs. Cabot and Chandler, architects, of Boston; and temporary quarters were secured in the building owned and formerly occupied by the Philadelphia Saving Fund Society, No. 306 Walnut street, now owned and occupied by the Royal Insurance Company, into which the company moved 24 May. On 12 July the old office submitted to the first stroke of destruction, and on 16 August, the first foundation-stone of the new building was laid on the Walnut street line. The winter of 1880 and 1881 came early, and proved an exceptionably severe one, and the work was much delayed. The following summer saw the completion of the present handsome and substantial building, and occupancy was finally enjoyed by the company on 6 December, 1881.

X.

LIVES OF THE FOUNDERS AND THE PRESIDENTS.

A HISTORY of the Insurance Company of North America would not be complete without fitting notices of its executive officers. A retrospect of the lives of these men will show the causes of the company's endurance through trying times, and its final established successes; representative men they all were, and their connection necessarily made the company a representative corporation. It has not been a light task to gather materials for their memoirs, but sufficient is now known of them, to recognize in them, men of parts, of intelligence, and of probity; and in some of them, men, who on behalf of their native country, took no common part in aiding its establishment as an independent nation; men who gave their best energies and of their means to their country, could not but be found faithful to the institution whose concerns were in after years committed to their care and oversight. Of Mr. Nesbitt, the first president, but little can now be gathered. To him, and especially to Mr. Hazard, must be granted the meed of the successful establishment of the company; hence, the ensuing notice of Mr. Hazard properly follows that of Mr. Nesbitt, before we can enter upon the public and private career of the latter's successor, Colonel Pettit. And a notice of Mr. Samuel Blodget, though he was not an officer, finds the most appropriate place as a co-founder with Mr. Hazard and the others immediately following that of Mr. Hazard.

1.

Mr. JOHN MAXWELL NESBITT was born in Ireland in 1728, and came to this country in early life, and entering mercantile life, became very successful in business, in the conduct of an extensive mercantile house in this city, which was widely known in its connections successively as that of Conyngham, Nesbitt & Co., the senior being Mr. Redmond Conyngham, who subsequently returned to Ireland, and there died, and whose advertisements appear in the *Pennsylvania Gazette* as early as 9 June, 1757; of John M. Nesbitt & Co.; and of Conyngham, Nesbitt & Co., when David Hayfield Conyngham, the son of Redmond, was admitted, and the old style was resumed. His interest in Colonial affairs led him into active participation in the Revolution, he and his younger partner Mr. Conyngham, being elected members of the First Troop Philadelphia City Cavalry in March, 1777, as his elder brother, Alexander Nesbitt had been two years preceding. He remained an active member of this now venerable company through the Revolution, sharing in its New Jersey campaigns, and on his resignation, was made an honorary member 10 September, 1787, with his brother.

Mr. Nesbitt was one of the original members of the Friendly Sons of St. Patrick, and was elected vice-president at their first meeting, 17 September, 1771. He became its second president in 1773, and afterwards held the same office from June, 1782 to March, 1796, at which time his

health began to fail. It was from the membership of this
society that the Hibernian Society was formed 27 June,
1792, a society which to this day continues in useful activity,
and is the heir to the good fame of the Friendly Sons. So
many of his associates in this organization warmly espoused
the side of the Colonies when the clouds of bitter dis-
appointment arose, shutting out hope of any redress of
grievances from the British parliament, that Mr. Nesbitt
would have been singular, had he forborne participation in
the stir of the times. On 17 June, 1780, the house of J.
M. Nesbitt & Co. subscribed £5,000 to the fund to support
the credit of a bank for furnishing a supply of provisions
for the use of the army, and Mr. Nesbitt was appointed one
of the five inspectors of the organization, which was effected
under the name of the "Pennsylvania Bank." Mr. Simpson
in his *Lives of Eminent Philadelphians*, narrates the story
of his faithful patriotism, when Judge Peters called on him
among the first after his receiving a letter from General
Washington, depicting the great needs and suffering of the
army, and explaining to him the wishes of Washington.
Mr. Nesbitt replied, "that a Mr. Howe, of Trenton, had
offered to put up pork for him if he were paid in hard
money, and that he had contracted with Howe to put up all
the pork and beef he could possibly obtain, for which he
should be paid in gold." The engagement was performed
by Mr. Howe, and J. M. Nesbitt & Co. paid him the gold.
Mr. Nesbitt said to Judge Peters he might have this beef
and pork, and, in addition, a valuable prize just arrived,
laden with provisions. Mr. Nesbitt, with others prominent
in the organization of the Bank of Pennsylvania, identified

themselves with the new banking institution promoted by Robert Morris the year following, and at the organization of the Bank of North America, on 1 November, 1781, he was elected one of its directors, and he continued in the board until 9 January, 1792. On 31 December following, it was incorporated as "The President, Directors, and Company of the Bank of North America," and here we may perhaps find the original of the title to the new insurance company which ten years later opened its doors under Mr. Nesbitt's presidency.

Judge Peters was one of the witnesses to his will, with James S. Ritchie, Francis West, and Redmond Conyngham, which was proved 25 January, 1802, and by which he left his entire estate, after providing annuities to his surviving brother James and three sisters, to his friend and partner Mr. Conyngham, whose son, the late Judge Conyngham, the eminent Pennsylvania jurist, born four years before his death, was named John Nesbitt Conyngham. In the *Daily Advertiser* of 27 January, 1802, a friend's obituary of Mr. Nesbitt describes him in the following words: "This worthy citizen maintained for upwards of half a century the character of an upright and intelligent merchant in this city. In his extensive dealings, friendship and kindness always tempered the claims of interest and justice. In private life he was truly amiable, and so circumspect and discreet in his manners, as never to offend by speech or conduct. His remains were interred on Sunday [24th] in the First Presbyterian Church, and attended by a numerous concourse of respectable friends and fellow citizens."

2.

MR. EBENEZER HAZARD was one of the earlier promoters of the association which gave birth to the Insurance Company of North America, and to his energy and industry must be largely attributed the instant success and the steady growth of the institution. He was a man of note among his peers, and prominent in all the various undertakings in which he engaged, and equally so in those initiated by others as in those of his own origination. The company was favored in having as it's first secretary so faithful and conscientious an officer, and one whose standing in business and literary circles allied him to a large connection, and whose wise administration of the general Post Office Department, for many years previously, was a guarantee to both its stockholders and its clients of a just administration of his responsible duties.

Ebenezer Hazard, the son of Samuel Hazard, of Philadelphia, who was the great-grandson of Thomas Hazard, who came from Wales and settled on Long Island, was born in that city 26 January, 1745, and "was baptised in the 'New Building' in Fourth street below Arch," later known as the Old Academy, on 7 February, by Rev. Gilbert Tennent. He was the second son, and named after the Rev. Ebenezer Pemberton, who was the pastor of his mother at the First Presbyterian Church, New York, and by whom his parents were married in October, 1739; she was the daughter of Matthew Clarkson, of that city, whose wife was Cornelia Depeyster, and the sister of Matthew Clarkson, who was in 1792 mayor of the city of Philadelphia. Samuel Hazard resided some years in New York,

Eben Hazard Sec^y

but returned to Philadelphia before the birth of his son.

He was a merchant, and sold books among his other merchandise, and was one of the founders of the Pennsylvania Hospital, and for a number of years a manager until his death; and an original and active trustee of the College of New Jersey, and was one of the first members of the Second Presbyterian Church, which was organized through the instrumentality of the Rev. George Whitefield in 1743, and under the pastoral care of the Rev. Gilbert Tennent. He died 14 July, 1758.

Ebenezer Hazard spent his early years at the school of the Rev. Dr. Samuel Finley (who afterwards married, for his second wife, Anna Clarkson, Hazard's aunt) at Nottingham, Maryland, and graduated at Princeton College in 1762, of which Dr. Finley had become the president the year previously; one of his classmates was Jonathan Dickinson Sergeant. In 1780 he wrote a life of Dr. Finley. In November, 1762, he enlisted in a privateer, and the following month was wrecked off Martinique; subsequently shipping on H. M. ship *Scarborough* he cruised in the West Indies until June, 1764, and afterwards sailing for England was there discharged and arrived home in March, 1765.

He removed to New York in 1767, and engaged there in the book business with Garret Noel, and in 1770 became his partner under the style of Noel & Hazard, and so continued until April, 1774, when the business proving less successful the firm was dissolved. It was in this connection that he developed that intimacy with books which was so helpful to him in after years, and made for him those

7

literary acquaintances which through life afforded him very agreeable connections.

He spent parts of the years 1770 and 1771 in England. In July, 1775, the New York Provincial Congress recommended him to the Continental Congress as a fit person for postmaster, and on 5 October he was appointed the first postmaster of New York. On 30 August, 1776, the day after the retreat of the American army from Long Island, he was ordered by the Committee of Safety to Dobbs Ferry, and in this neighborhood the New York post office mostly remained until after the evacuation of the city by the British army in November, 1783. In 1777 he was appointed surveyor of the post roads and offices throughout the country, and traveled on duty on horseback between New Hampshire and Georgia until his appointment 28 January, 1782, as Postmaster General of the United States. He was the third to fill this office, in which he continued for seven years, succeeding Richard Bache who had succeeded Benjamin Franklin. It was at this period he writes "he is hurried through life on horseback," but his new appointment gives him promise of a settled place of residence—which he found in his native city. It was in 1779, in the midst of his wanderings on government service, that he began to gather materials for his *Historical Collections, consisting of State Papers and other Authentic Documents intended as materials for a History of the United States,* no doubt filling in his spare moments in his tours through the principal towns by copying documents and manuscripts, which he finally published, the first volume in 1792 and the second in 1794. It was with his usual untiring industry that being armed by the authority of Congress with the right to examine and copy whatever he saw fit, that he made copies of State papers and documents which he observed were fast going to decay or were being scattered and lost. Dr. Allibone truly says of him and his son Samuel, the compiler of the *Colonial Records of Pennsylvania* and the *Pennsylvania Archives*, that "it is to such indefatigable laborers that historians are indebted for much of the most valuable portions of their compilations." His labors on this work were in part interrupted by his appointment as Postmaster General, but were resumed in 1789 on his retirement and then pursued to completion, though the second volume was published when he was engrossed in his very active duties as secretary of the Insurance Company of North America.

Mr. Hazard married, 11 September, 1783, Abigail, daughter of Joseph and Jane (Chevalier) Arthur of Nantucket. They were married at the residence of Judge Breese, in Shrewsbury, N. J., whose wife was Mrs. Hazard's elder half-sister; Judge Breese by his first marriage with Rev. Dr. Finley's daughter became the grandfather of the great inventor Samuel F. B. Morse, LL. D. In his correspondence with Dr. Jeremy Belknap, whose *History of New Hampshire* was published in Philadelphia in 1784 under the superintendence of Mr. Hazard, there are many interesting personal references to the Breese family and its connections; this correspondence was published by the Massachusetts Historical Society in 1878, and evidences Mr. Hazard's business as well as literary ability, and affords us a good exposition of his christian and manly character as well as his merits as a finished letter-writer.

He began his housekeeping on Arch street, old No. 161, below Fifth street, where their son Samuel was born 26 May, 1784; but on the removal of Congress to New York his office followed, and he renewed his residence in that city, and there continued until his retirement from office in 1789. Charles Thomson, the secretary of Congress, writes his wife from New York, 6 April, 1785: "Hazard, the postmaster-general, has in consequence of the order of Congress come here and has been trying to get a house. He meets with difficulty, and wishes to have leave to reside in Philadelphia; whether he will get leave or not I cannot tell."—*MS. letter.* He finally returned to Philadelphia in December, 1790, having in that year served on the board of three, appointed by General Knox, Secretary of War, to appraise West Point, then about to be purchased by the government. He here entered into the brokerage of stocks with Jonas Addoms, a firm which continued until 1792. He may have united the brokerage of insurances in his business, which doubtless brought him in connection with the project broached early in the latter year, of forming in Philadelphia an Association of Underwriters.

He was the owner of two lots and houses on Arch street above Fourth street, one of which he had purchased in 1783, and in April, 1792, he removed these and erected on the eastern portion of this property his three-story brick mansion, No. 145 Arch street (now 415), into which he moved in November. He describes it to Dr. Belknap as "a fair brick house in an inconvenient part of the city, and too remote from the theatre of business." This was sold by his executrix on 8 November, 1817, to William Sansom, who purchased it for his daughter, Mrs. George Vaux, and until its purchase and destruction by Mr. Womrath in 1861 it was generally known as the Vaux Mansion; the eastern of the three buildings erected by Mr. Womrath stands on part of the site of the old house; the remainder of the lot was thrown into the garden; adjoining on the west was Mr. John Cooke's property, which was also purchased by Mr. Womrath, and upon these two his three stores are erected. This mansion which Mr. Hazard built, which he occupied for twenty-five years, and therein died, is of interest as containing the office of the North America, and where all its business was transacted during the prevalence of the fearful epidemic of yellow fever in 1793, as the regular office had to be abandoned on account of its vicinity to the affected district. He writes 12 October, 1793, to his friend, S. A. Otis, "Here I am, with my family, in the midst of disease and death, which will no doubt surprise many, but Divine Providence had placed me in such a situation that it appeared evidently to be my duty to remain in town. This point being settled, I had no difficulty in determining what to do. I have always found the path of duty to be the way of safety; and whilst I know that I walk in it, I can cheerfully commit all events to the Great Disposer of them." And on 30 October to Dr. Jeremy Belknap he writes: "To remove from the city, or not, was early a question in my mind; but upon thinking over all circumstances, and especially how much depended on me respecting the insurance office, I felt it to be my duty to remain in the city, and determined accordingly. I have not been out at all, and Mrs. Hazard would not have me, so we all took our

chance together." These extracts testify to the steadfast-
ness and faithfulness of the man, who believed his way of
safety was in the path of duty. The president, Mr. Nesbitt,
a man not of robust health, had early left the city and found
refuge at his partner Mr. Conyngham's residence. Clermont,
three miles to the north of the city, and from there communicated almostly daily with Mr. Hazard. But the
epidemic invaded his household, and he and Mrs. Hazard,
his daughter, his sister, a young woman from the country,
a servant, and man were all in succession stricken down,
and his sister Anna died of it 18 October, and was buried
the same day, and the old servant was also a victim to it.
In his letter to Mr. Otis of 12 October he says: "We have
had our share of the disorder, but it has been very moderate
compared with the sufferings of others. I am recovered;
Mrs. Hazard is so well as to be about the house."

On 27 July he had written Dr. Belknap: "I am seldom
with my family, except at meal times and while I am asleep,
and frequently do not leave the office before nine at night.
Perhaps I perform works of supererogation, but it seems to
be necessary at present. If business continues to encrease
as it has done, assistance will be necessary." His industry
appeared to be exceptional; all the records of the office
were kept by him for many months; books, correspondence
and policies were all from his pen, and he personally attended
to all minutiæ of the office; for though a clerk was in a
short time after the company's operations began employed,
all the responsible clerical work remained in his hands.
The office work of those days was prolonged, and while
to-day we condense in a few consecutive hours the work of

the entire day, the custom of the period was to accommo-
date the merchants, who mainly living over their counting-
houses had no limits of hours in the transaction of their
private or business affairs. We find that by resolution of
the directors on 15 January, 1795, the president was
required to attend the office from eleven to two o'clock, and
five to eight, and the secretary from ten to two, and from
four to eight each day. This practice continued in effect
for nine years. On 18 July, 1797, Mr. Hazard writes Dr.
Belknap, "It is not necessary that our hours of business
should be such as they are, and I have tried to get them
altered so as to give me a little time for recreation, but I have
not succeeded." On 14 January, 1796, he writes: "It is
near Ten O'clock at night and I have not left the office
yet." And it was in the midst of this labor, that he passed
through the press the second volume of his *Historical
Collections*, for which he was obliged to prepare a second
Index, as his first MS. of this was destroyed at the fire of
Thomas Dobson's, the publisher.

Correlative to Mr. Hazard's industrious and faithful
application to his duties in the North America, it is well to
quote here his account of his labors as Postmaster General
recounted in his address to President Washington, 21
September, 1789, when a change seemed to be impending
in the management of the office. "Though I have made
repeated applications for more assistance and so clearly
pointed out the necessity there was for it, that a Committee
of Congress reported in favor of its being allowed, I have
been left to encounter the whole business of the department
almost alone. * * Besides the general superin-

tendence of fifteen hundred miles, exclusive of post roads,
I have had to maintain a very burthensome correspondence;
to examine the quarterly returns from all the eastern offices;
to enter all the accounts; to keep the books of the department (which since my appointment has been in double
entry); to make communications to Congress and committees, which have frequently required lengthy and tedious
calculations; to form and enter into contracts, and pay the
contractors quarterly; to inspect the dead letters; and to
do the business out of doors as well as within. My own
attention has been so constantly necessary that I have not
had time for proper relaxation, and in three years past,
have not been to the distance of ten miles from this city.
I once hired a clerk, but found my salary was not equal to
that expense in addition to the support of my family, and
was obliged to dismiss him."   It was under his administration that the department for the first time became paying.

Mr. Hazard's pecuniary interests in the company were
great, and many of the stockholders were his personal
friends. Mr. Robert Ralston, whose wife was his cousin, was
a director until 1800. On 17 December, 1799, he asks leave
to resign, as his health was so much affected by his constant
close attention to business, and the same year he appears
to have parted with the major part of his stock and at a
handsome premium; and at the stockholders' meeting on
13 January following, his resignation was accepted with
their "thanks for his long and faithful services as secretary
of this company."   He was requested to act as secretary
pro tem. until the office was supplied, but he did not
continue this long; a temporary arrangement was made by

which Mr. Robert S. Stephens, the bookkeeper should be first clerk and to countersign checks, but no secretary was appointed until Mr. Stephens' election to the office 28 February, 1806. It was during the last years of his administration that occurred the heavy drains upon the company's fund from the captures of our merchantmen by French cruisers, amounting in the aggregate to the sum of $514,125.80, and the harassments arising from this source with the uncertainty of the company being reimbursed by the French government, contributed greatly to Mr. Hazard's desire to be released from any further official responsibility. In his seven years' secretaryship, the company had in its marine business received in premiums $4,588,497.29, and paid in losses $3,556,682.99, and in its fire business, begun in December, 1794, had received $49,241.26 premiums, and paid losses $22,853.99, and upon its capital of $600,000, had paid dividends to its stockholders amounting to $591,296.63.

But Mr. Hazard's energies forbade idleness, and his release from office duties allowed him opportunities for equally efficient work in philanthropic and literary pursuits and in ecclesiastical stations. He was trustee and elder in the Second Presbyterian Church, then at Third and Arch streets, from 1784 until his death, and was trustee of the General Assembly; during his residence in New York, he had been a trustee of the First Presbyterian Church, located in Wall street. He was a deeply read bible student, and a fine Greek scholar, and revised Charles Thomson's MSS. of his original translation of the bible. The correspondence between the two is yet preserved in the family, and Thomson generally yielded to the reasons advanced by Mr. Hazard for his corrections. He finally purchased Mr. Thomson's share in the transaction, and afterwards disposed of it to Earle, the bookseller, and as it was passing through the press in 1808 he corrected the proof-sheets. He was Curator of the American Philosophical Society, to which he often contributed papers; the first corresponding member of the Massachusetts Historical Society; member of the New York Historical Society, and fellow of the American Academy of Natural Sciences. He was for many years manager of the Schuylkill and Pennsylvania Bridge Company; of the Delaware and Schuylkill Canal Company; of the Philadelphia Dispensary; a member of the Guardians of the Poor; and of the Board of Missions. He was the author of the proposals and the outline of the act for the Schuylkill Navigation Company, which was incorporated in 1813. He was a useful promoter, with his influence and capital, of many local improvements, and while possessing a sound judgment in all things, he was of such liberal and enterprising turn of mind, that he ever stood ready to take a share of the risk which any venture that was sanctioned by his judgment demanded. But no greater monument exists to his memory in financial affairs than the Insurance Company which had the impulse of his mind in the outstart, and his steadfast and faithful administration in its years of infancy; and the same business soundness and executive ability in the successive officers of the company will preserve to it the like favoring success which he so firmly established.

Mr. Hazard died at his residence on Arch street, on 13 April, 1817, and was buried in the ground on the north side

of Arch street, west of Fifth street; but on the removal
of that cemetery, his remains were taken to Laurel Hill.
His widow survived him a few years, dying 6 July, 1820.
Mr. Hazard had four children, the youngest dying in
infancy. The eldest, was Samuel, born 26 May, 1784, whose
name is established in American historic annals as one of
its most indefatigable compilers, and who died 26 May,
1870; the second, was Elizabeth Breese, who married first
Ebenezer Rockwood, of Boston, and secondly, the Rev.
Thomas E. Vermilye, D.D., of New York, and died in
1861, aged 75 years; and the third, was Erskine, born 30
November, 1789, who was identified with the development
of the Pennsylvania anthracite coal fields, and was one of
the originators of the Lehigh Navigation Company, of which
he was for many years the president, and as well was interested in the promotion of other enterprises to develop the
iron as well as coal business of his native State. He died in
1865.*

3.

Mr. SAMUEL BLODGET, Jr. was a native of Woburn,
Massachusetts, where he was born in 1755. He entered
into military service and passed three years' arduous duty,
part of the time on the staff of General Washington, whom
he had first met at the encampment at Cambridge in 1775,
and with whom his father was personally intimate. Subsequently, he engaged in the East India trade, and made
visits to Europe in 1784 and 1790. He married for his

* See sketch by Mr. Willis P. Hazard of his grandfather's life in Mr. Thomas
R. Hazard's *Recollections of Olden Times*, New York, 1879.

second wife, on 10 May, 1792. Rebecca, the second daughter
of the Reverend William Smith, D.D., Provost of the
University of Pennsylvania. Mr. Blodget was a man of
bold spirit and venture, and while interesting himself in the
Tontine Association, and equally in its successor the Insurance Company, he continued his efforts to found the national
capital, a scheme he had been formulating for some years,
and which took shape on his last return from Europe; and
in connection with this, he planned a National University,
the details of which he had studied out in his foreign tours,
and in the interests of which he frequently conferred with
Dr. Smith, which led to an intimacy in his family, resulting
in the marriage with his daughter. In his *Economica, a
statistical Manual for the United States of America*,* he
says of himself: "The writer needed not the recommendation of his former commander to persuade him to purchase,
as he did in 1791, property to the amount of above $100,000
in and adjoining the city, one day to become the noblest of
the universe." His plans for the new city embraced the
establishment of his university, which was "what he most
prized, designed in part at the Hague, and completed at
Oxford, where he had all the universities of ancient and
modern times to guide his pencil." The success of the new
city of Washington was due to his skill and management,
though some measure of the profits of his investments are
realized only at this late day by his descendants of the third
generation. Mr. Blodget died in Philadelphia, 11 April,
1814, and was buried on the 13th, in Christ Church burying-

---

* 1813, 14 April, the directors subscribe for one copy Samuel Blodget's Statistical Works. This copy yet remains in the company's library.

Cha. Pettit. Pres.

ground, but no stone marks the grave of the founder of Washington City.

4.

COLONEL CHARLES PETTIT, son of John Pettit, was born near Amwell, New Jersey, in 1737. He was early trained in public affairs. While a young man at Trenton, Perth Amboy, Burlington and New Brunswick, in the Province of New Jersey, he held positions in connection with the Courts of the Province under the Provincial Government of George III. His earliest commission appears to be one dated 27 October, 1769, as Deputy Secretary, Clerk of the Council, Clerk of the Supreme Court, Clerk of the Pleas, Surrogate, and Keeper and Register of the Records of the Province. During this period he also held commission dated 8 March, 1771, as Aide-de-Camp, with rank of Lieut. Colonel, to William Franklin, Governor of the Province; and after Franklin's arrest in 1776, he was commissioned at Princeton 8 October, 1776 as Aide-de-Camp, with rank of Colonel, to Governor William Livingston.

He was Colonial Secretary under Governor Franklin, and held most intimate and constant intercourse with him during the last eventful years of his administration. After the revolutionary proceedings of the Colonial Legislature of New Jersey, which brought to a close the Franklin administration, Colonel Charles Pettit was again appointed Secretary of the Province by Governor Livingston. In the published records and archives of the Province of New

Jersey, we find his name frequently given in connection
with proceedings of the executive and of the Provincial
Congress previous to 1776. His residence had been at
Burlington, but he removed with his family to Perth Amboy
in 1774 when Governor Franklin removed thither; when
Franklin was taken prisoner in 1776, he appears subsequently to have made his residence in Philadelphia, after
a short service as Secretary of the Province. During this
period, fraught with anxiety to every lover of liberty in the
Colonies, we find that Colonel Pettit continually co-operated
to promote harmony between the Colony and the mother
country, and if possible, by means lawful and peaceful and
honorable alike both to England and the Province, prevent
that trouble, resort to arms, which the obstinacy of the
King and his Privy Council finally rendered necessary.

In the eventful year 1776, being forty years of age, we find
him providing for the safety and protection of the records
of the Province, which the Assembly of New Jersey by
special act of legislation had put into his charge. And subsequently he entered the military service of his country, being
commissioned Assistant Quartermaster-General to Major-
General Greene on the latter's appointment 2 March, 1778.*
In this latter capacity he rendered faithful, efficient and
responsible service for a long period under General Greene,
and was with him at White Plains, Philadelphia and elsewhere. With General Greene he had maintained an intimate
friendship since childhood, and when that officer resigned,

---

*At the same time Col. John Cox was appointed assistant quartermaster-
general, and General Greene said "nothing could have induced him to accept
this post but the appointment of those two gentlemen as his aids." See letter
to General Reed, 9 March, 1778.

Colonel Pettit was offered the Quartermaster-General-ship, but declined it.

About 1783 he moved permanently to Philadelphia, and soon thereafter became engaged in mercantile pursuits. Here he was at once again thrown into public life.

He entered the Pennsylvania Legislature in July, 1784, and in the Continental Congress, to which he was elected the next year, serving from 7 April, 1785 for two years. During this term of service the great questions relative to the organization of the Republic, by the adoption of a Constitution for the Confederation of States, were engross-ing the attention of all those patriots who strove to place upon a firm and lasting basis that independence for which they had risked their lives and fortunes. One of Colonel Pettit's contemporaries has thus recorded this position in regard to this matter, as follows: "He stated his objections to certain portions of the document with firmness, but recommended its adoption with candour, and it is known that he became the principal instrument of subduing the Pennsylvania opposition by his conciliatory conduct at the general conference which was held in Harrisburg previously to the ultimate vote of ratification." On 13 April, 1791, he was appointed the commissioner to superin-tend accounts of the Commonwealth with the National government; and was the author of the funding system of Pennsylvania. He was a trustee of the University of Pennsylvania from 1791 to 1802, and a member of the American Philosophical Society, to which he had been elected 21 January, 1785, in whose deliberations he took a lively part.

One of the original directors of the North America, and an intimate friend of Mr. Hazard, Colonel Pettit was active in its interests and zealous in promoting its growth; and on the resignation of Mr. Nesbitt, he was on 13 January, 1796, unanimously elected president. In September of the following year, he met with an accident while driving with his friend General Jonathan Williams, near the latter's seat, Mount Pleasant, which so seriously affected his health, that on his urgent request, the directors finally accepted his resignation on 9 January, 1798. On his illness it became necessary to appoint a president *pro tem.*, and Mr. Joseph Ball was elected, who was eventually appointed president in January following. The office of the company was at this time in Arch street, and the members, in fear of the yellow fever, were out of the city; and we find an entry in the cash book on 17 September of a payment to "J. Hardy for horse hire, occasioned in calling a Board of Directors to a special meeting to elect a president *pro tem.*" Colonel Pettit's health was regained, though he was permanently lamed, and his interest in company affairs was renewed, and on Mr. Ball declining further to serve on account of the office taking more of his time than he could spare from his private affairs, he was re-elected 8 July, 1799, and continued in office until his death, 3 September, 1806. The board had granted him the use of two rooms in the upper part of their office-building southwest corner Front and Walnut, when they removed thither in December, 1797, in consideration of his infirmities, and here he dwelt during Mr. Ball's presidency, and on his re-election, their use to him was continued, or as the minutes quaintly express it, "he was indulged (rent free) on account of indisposition, with such part of the building not rented." He continued his residence here until the office was removed to No. 98 south Second street, when he moved his rooms to Dock street, near Second street, where he died. An obituary to his memory appeared in the *Daily Advertiser*, 9 September, 1806, the authorship of which is attributed to the pen of his friend General Williams, whereby we can form a truer estimate of the man's character and influence, than by the mere recital of his various public duties. His interest in the company descends to present generations of his family; his only son, Andrew, was a director thirty-two years; his son-in-law, Andrew Bayard, from 1798 to 1805, and his great-grandson, Thomas Charlton Henry, elected a director in 1864, was on 2 November, 1880, elected vice-president of the company, and the latter's grandfather, Alexander Henry, an intimate friend of Colonel Pettit, had been a director for the extended term of forty-eight years. Colonel Pettit married 5 April, 1758, Sarah, daughter of Andrew Reed* of Trenton, by his first wife, and was thus intimately connected with General Joseph Reed, the son, by Mr. Reed's second marriage. With William Bradford and Jared Ingersoll he was an executor of the will of General Joseph Reed, who died 5 March,

---

* Colonel Pettit's father and father-in-law had been associated as Reed & Pettit, in general merchandising in Philadelphia; and we have their advertisement in the *Pennsylvania Gazette*, 7 August, 1760, "at their store in Front Street, a few doors below Walnut Street, directly opposite Mr. William West's," nigh to the building in which the first office of the Insurance Company of North America was opened. Reed & Pettit were among the prominent underwriters of Philadelphia, for we find the firm subscribing to marine policies in respectable amounts as early as in July, 1759, as shown by Walter Shee's books, and as late as November, 1762, we find them in Kidd & Bradford's books.

8

1785. Colonel Pettit's children were a son Andrew, and three daughters: Elizabeth, who married Jared Ingersoll, the eminent member of the Philadelphia bar, and for many years the counsellor of the Insurance Company of North America; Sarah, who married Andrew Bayard, and Theodosia, who married Alexander Graydon, the author of *Graydon's Memoirs*.

Portraits of Colonel Pettit were made by Gilbert Stuart and Charles Willson Peale; it is from the former's painting that the cut is taken which is produced here.

5.

MR. JOSEPH BALL was born in Douglas township, Berks county, Pennsylvania, in 1752, the son of John and Mary (Richards) Ball. In early manhood he became manager of the iron works at Batsto, Burlington county, New Jersey, then owned by Colonel John Cox; this was in the earlier years of the Revolution, and in 1779 he became the proprietor. These works were extensively employed in the manufacture of shot and shells for the Continental service. The correspondence of Mr. Ball and Colonel Cox with the Committee of Safety of Philadelphia in May, 1776, given in the *Pennsylvania Archives*, 1st series, 4th volume, shows that the ammunition then being furnished to the committee was by their special order, hauled by teams from Batsto to Cooper's ferry, now Camden, instead of being transported by the usual less expeditious mode of conveyance by water. Mr. Ball took the oath of allegiance to Pennsylvania 10 September, 1777, and during the Revolution he was an active patriot and advanced liberally of his means in aid of the cause. He entered into business in Philadelphia and with much success accumulating a goodly fortune and becoming largely interested in real estate. After the close of the war, it is said he embarked in the schemes for the restoration of the public credit inaugurated by Robert Morris, by means of which he with many others suffered much pecuniary loss. He was, in October, 1791, elected a director of the Bank of the United States, which Congress had incorporated in the month of February previous; and he was one of the original board of the Insurance Company of North America, and was influential in its councils; during an absence of Mr. Nesbitt he acted as president *pro tem.* in February, 1794, when Colonel Pettit met with his severe accident, he was on 20 September, 1797 again made president *pro tem.*, and on 9 January following, on Colonel Pettit's resignation, was elected president. His private affairs, however, were many and pressing, and he resigned his office 8 July, 1799. His seat in the board was declared vacant 1 August, 1803, under the charter, agreeably to the provision formerly recited, to the effect that a director of the company could not act or serve in like capacity in another insurance company, as he had taken part in the organization of the Union Insurance Company and on 26 July preceding, had been elected its first president. This company was chartered 6 February, 1804, and Mr. Ball continued president until 10 February, 1807, when he declined re-election and was succeeded by Mr. George Latimer. His country seat was on Point-no-Point road, the site now being merged in the improvements of the Reading Railroad

Company at Port Richmond. Here he died 2 September, 1825, leaving a large property, which upon the death of his wife, and leaving no children, was divided among a large number of heirs. He was first cousin to Mr. Benjamin W. Richards, who was mayor of the city of Philadelphia from 1829 to 1832.

6.

Mr. JOHN INSKEEP was elected a director in 1802, and on Colonel Pettit's death was elected president 1 October, 1806. He was born near Marlton, Burlington county, New Jersey, 29 January, 1757. He took part in the Revolutionary struggle, and was Commissary of Issues at one time, and captain in the second battalion Gloucester militia. Subsequently coming to Philadelphia, he became proprietor of the George Inn, at the southwest corner of Dock and Second streets, and afterwards entered the China trade and became a prosperous merchant, and was active in many public enterprises. He was elected mayor of the city in 1800, and again in 1804 and 1805, and became president of the company at the close of the last term. He had also served as alderman in 1801 and 1802. His conduct of the presidency of the company was very successful, and in July, 1824 the board voted him a set of plate valued at $500, as an acknowledgment of his services in procuring the reimbursement of the claims under the Spanish treaty, which produced to the stockholders, as stated on a former page, a dividend of sixty per cent. at that semi-annual period. He acknowledges receipt of this worthy testimonial

FOURTH PRESIDENT 1806-1851.

on 19 August following, in a well-written letter, which is retained in the company files. In his will (proved 23 December, 1834) he directs that "the plate presented to me by the Insurance Company of North America, over which I presided, be divided equally between them [his children] or as nearly so in point of value as the pieces of which it is composed will admit." He resigned the presidency, due to increasing infirmities, 5 April, 1831, the directors voting him an annuity "until otherwise ordered," which was only terminated by his death 18 December, 1834. He is buried in Christ Church burying-ground, Fifth and Arch streets. The children named in his will were Abraham H., Mrs. Samuel Fisher Bradford, Mrs. Samuel Brooks and Mrs. Robert Taylor. His wife was Sarah Hewlings, whom he married in 1776, and who surviving him, died 17 January, 1842. She was in receipt of a pension from the government for her husband's services in the Revolution. A son John, who died before him, was taken in partnership by Mr. Bradford, his brother-in-law, forming the well-known and eminent firm of Bradford & Inskeep, publishers and booksellers of this city.

7.

Mr. JOHN CORREY SMITH was born in Philadelphia, 3 October, 1784, the son of Dr. William Smith, an eminent druggist. He early engaged in mercantile pursuits, and for many years was actively and successfully engaged in the China trade. He was elected a director in January, 1831, and president 5 April following. He died suddenly 22 June,

1845. The *United States Gazette* on the following day noticed his death and said: "Mr. Smith during his long life fulfilled the duties which elevate and distinguish the man and the merchant, with such propriety, and with such efficiency, that he gained consideration for his worth, and respect where respect was so difficult of attainment and valuable in a commensurate degree. He was for many years one of the first merchants of our city, and at the period of his decease, was the president of the North American Insurance Company, a post he filled with much ability." His sons are Harrison, Cooper and Charles Ross Smith, merchants of this city; and his brother, Samuel F. Smith, served two terms in the Direction of the company from 1830 to 1835 and 1838 to 1862, thirty-one years in all, dying 23 August, 1862, aged eighty four years; he was also president, during the latter term, of the Philadelphia National Bank from 1842 to 1852.

8.

Mr. Arthur Gilman Coffin was born October, 1799, in Gloucester, Massachusetts, the son of Dr. William Coffin, a prominent physician of that place and a descendant of Tristam Coffin, one of the eight original purchasers and pioneer settlers of Nantucket. After full preparatory training at the celebrated Phillip's Academy in Exeter, N. H., he entered Harvard College but did not complete his studies there, owing to his father's death, and came to Philadelphia about 1824. Here he soon found employment,

John C. Smith

entering the shipping house of Messrs. Havens & Smith, where he won the confidence and esteem of all, and when a vacancy occurred in the secretaryship of the Insurance Company of North America he was induced to make application for it, which was strongly endorsed. His letter of application, yet preserved in the company's files, is indicative of the directness and simplicity of the man.

He was elected secretary 19 June, 1832, against strong competitors, and fulfilled the duties of his office with such faithfulness and skill during almost the entire administration of President Smith, that on the death of that gentleman he was unanimously elected president 1 July, 1845. His administration proved an eventful one, and marked the growth of the company up to the requirements of modern usages in both marine and fire underwriting; his good judgment and kindly tact effected a gradual change in the management of the responsibilities of the business which he found largely assumed by the directors through their weekly committees, which system gradually failed of active operations not only from the growing weight of the business, but as well also from the entire confidence the board grew to place in his equitable and conservative administration. A perusal of the minutes during this period show the gradual reference of important matters to the president "with power" for his final action; and this position was attained by the influence of his great modesty and deference, for he continued to refer to the board matters of detail even after the practice had grown up of leaving all to his decision. He was a just man and an intelligent underwriter; his professional opinions always had great weight, and his practical wisdom gave him an influence among all classes of men with whom he associated allotted to but few. When he assumed the presidency, the year closed with a capital of $300,000, and total assets of $426,507.84. The year of his resignation found the capital of the company $2,000,000, and the assets, $6,461,729.70. For some years his health had been failing, and while deprived of steady participation in the conduct of the affairs of the company, he never withheld hearty endorsement to all the growing activities of the company, and its growth in wealth and position afforded him keen gratification. He desired to withdraw from the presidency, and the board declined to listen to his appeal; until finally he pressed the matter, and his resignation was finally accepted on 14 January, 1878. But in thus parting from him as president, he still remained a director, and the board continued to him his remaining years, a practical acknowledgment of their debt to his wise and faithful administration. He lived but a few years after; physically weak, and becoming more infirm, but busying himself in kindly thought with all the interests he had been connected with in his active life. Added to his office duties, he was for a third of a century vestryman of St. Andrew's Church, and some time warden; for many years a member of the Board of Education, and by the election of Councils, a director of Girard College. He was a member of the first board of managers of the Merchants' Fund Association, and for a quarter of a century a member and the chairman of its executive committee; and during the same period he was a manager of the Union Benevolent Association, and

Arthur G. Coffin

SIXTH PRESIDENT, 1843-1878.

also of the House of Refuge; for over forty years he was manager and president of the Magdalen Society; he was manager for more than a third of a century of the Pennsylvania Bible Society; and for many years a manager of the Pennsylvania Seaman's Friend Society. His death, 29 July, 1881, was felt far and wide, and both in corporate and private circles all recognized the loss as that of a christian friend and a safe counsellor.

9.

MR. CHARLES PLATT was born in the city of Philadelphia, the son of William and Maria (Taylor) Platt, on 16 February, 1829. After pursuing an academic course, he entered the University of Pennsylvania where he graduated with honor in 1846. The connections of his father's house with the China trade opened to him an early opportunity of entering into business. The year after his graduation he was sent to China in one of his father's ships, the *Tartar*, where he was trained in mercantile duties in the house of Ritchie & Co. at Canton. After passing three years here, he left for the United States, journeying in Calcutta and the Red Sea, and making the tour of Europe, reaching home in the autumn of 1850. In the following January he was admitted a partner in the house of William Platt & Sons. The large extensions of this eminent firm in the China and California trade and in the ownership of clipper ships, came to an end in the year 1854. For some years, as the junior partner, his time was given to settling up the affairs of the firm, and on 3 January, 1860, he was elected secretary of the Insurance Company of North America, and on 13 January, 1869, its vice-president, and finally on Mr. Coffin's resignation, was elected president 14 January, 1878.

Mr. Platt on his entrance upon the company's work in 1860, soon won the esteem and respect of the board composed of men his seniors in years, and in the trying years in the country's history which followed, was skilful and firm in the development of the company's business in all its branches, in which he had the hearty support and confidence of his venerated predecessor. His administration has covered the most active and growing period in the company's history, and the measures thereunder pursued have brought the company to the foremost rank of American institutions; in its fire branch to a national reputation, and in its marine branch to cosmopolitan renown. Of the directors serving on his election in 1860, only Messrs. Harrison and Cope survive.

APPENDIX.

(123)

AUTOGRAPH OF JOHN M. NESBITT, FIRST PRESIDENT, 1792-1796.

AUTOGRAPH OF JOSEPH BALL, THIRD PRESIDENT, 1798-1796.

1.

LIST OF OFFICERS, WITH THEIR TERMS OF SERVICE.

PRESIDENTS.

I.	JOHN M. NESBITT,	11 December, 1792–13 January, 1796.
II.	CHARLES PETTIT,	13 January, 1796–9 January, 1798.
III.	JOSEPH BALL,	9 January, 1798–8 July, 1799.
	CHARLES PETTIT,	8 July, 1799–3 September, 1806.
IV.	JOHN INSKEEP,	1 October, 1806–5 April, 1831.
V.	JOHN C. SMITH,	5 April, 1831–22 June, 1845.
VI.	ARTHUR G. COFFIN,	1 July, 1845–14 January, 1878.
VII.	CHARLES PLATT,	14 January, 1878.

VICE-PRESIDENTS.

I.	CHARLES PLATT,	13 January, 1869–14 January, 1878.
II.	T. CHARLTON HENRY,	2 November, 1880.

ACTING VICE-PRESIDENT.

WILLIAM S. DAVIS,	4 June, 1878–5 October, 1880.

(125)

SECOND VICE-PRESIDENTS.

I. William S. Davis, ... 3 March, 1874–5 October, 1880.

II. William A. Platt, . 12 January, 1881.

TREASURER.

Thomas H. Montgomery.
  Elected 23 November, 1880; declined, having accepted vice-presidency of the American Fire
  Insurance Company.

SECRETARIES.

I. Ebenezer Hazard, . . . 11 December, 1792–13 January, 1800.

II. Robert S. Stephens, ... 28 February, 1806–12 June, 1832.
  Bookkeeper, 27 February, 1798. First clerk, 21 January, 1800, to countersign checks.
  Resigns, 5 April, 1805, his clerkship.

III. Arthur G. Coffin, ... 19 June, 1832–1 July, 1845.

IV. Henry D. Sherrerd, ... 1 July, 1845–1 June, 1858.
  Secretary Atlantic Insurance Company, 17 July, 1857.
  President Insurance Company of the State of Pennsylvania, 28 May, 1858.

V. Matthias Maris, . . 2 November, 1858–3 April, 1860.

VI. Charles Platt, ... 3 April, 1860–26 January, 1869.

  Matthias Maris, ... 26 January, 1869–12 January, 1881.

VII. Greville E. Fryer, ... 12 January, 1881.

ASSISTANT SECRETARIES.

I. Alexander M. Walker, . . . 1 July, 1845–20 February, 1847.
  Clerk, 30 October, 1838.

II. Matthias Maris, ... 23 February, 1847–2 November, 1858.
  First Assistant—3 April, 1860–26 January, 1869.
  Clerk, 4 January, 1847.

III. F. P. Hollingshead. . . 29 November, 1859–9 February, 1864.

IV. Charles H. Reeves, . 10 August, 1869–14 January, 1874.

V. Greville E. Fryer, . 14 January, 1874–12 January, 1881.

VI. Eugene L. Ellison, ... 16 January, 1884.

LIST OF DIRECTORS, WITH THEIR TERMS OF SERVICE.

DIRECTORS.

106. ADAMS, ROBERT, . .	1807, 1808.	
140. ALLIBONE, S. AUSTIN.	1847–1857.	
119. ARCHER, SAMUEL. .	1816–1828.	Died 1839, aged 67.
55. ASH, JAMES.	1800–1804.	Died 24 Jan., 1830.
86. ASHLEY, JOHN.	1803.	
142. ASPINWALL, GEORGE W. .	1851–1853.	Died 1854, aged 40.
110. ASTLEY, THOMAS. . .	1809–1839.	
58. BAKER, JOHN H., .	1801.	
2. BALL, JOSEPH, .	1792–1803.	Died 2 September, 1825, aged 73. Third president, 2 January, 1798 to 8 July, 1799.
15. BARCLAY, JOHN,	1792, 1793.	
45. BAYARD, ANDREW.	1798–1805.	Died 1 June, 1832, aged 71.
42. BELL, THOMAS,	1797–1800.	
121. BEVAN, MATTHEW L. .	1822–1841.	
23. BLIGHT, PETER,	1794–1800.	Died 1812.
1. BLODGET, SAMUEL,	1792–1799.	Died 11 April, 1814, aged 59.
31. BRECK, SAMUEL,	1795–1797.	Died 7 May, 1809.
97. BOGGS, JAMES, .	1805–1808.	

141.	BOWEN, WILLIAM E..	1848–1866.	{ Died 17 April, 1866, aged 68.
157.	BROCKIE, WILLIAM.	1870–	
130.	BROOKS, SAMUEL. .	1835–1853.	Died 1853, aged 75.
93.	BROWN, ISRAEL.	1803.	
123.	BROWN, JOHN A., .	1828–1872.	{ Died 31 December, 1872, aged 84.
169.	BROWN, JOHN A., .	1881–	
105.	BROWN, JOHN H., .	1807–1816.	
171.	BUCKLEY, EDWARD S.	1882–	
116.	CARROW, JOHN G.,	1811–1813.	
131.	CHALONER, WILLIAM.	1836–1838.	{ Died 1 April, 1858, aged 71.
73.	CLAPIER, LEWIS, .	1802, 1803.	{ Died 4 May, 1837, aged 73.
149.	CLARKE, EDWARD S . .	1862–	
175.	COATES, EDWARD H.. .	1885–	
138.	COFFIN, ARTHUR G., .	1846–1881.	{ Died 29 July, 1881, aged 90. Third secretary, 19 June, 1852. Sixth president, 1 July, 1845 to 14 January, 1878.
59.	COMEGYS, CORNELIUS, .	1801–1804.	
36.	CONYNGHAM, DAVID H . .	1796–1800.	Died 5 March, 1831.
147.	COPE, FRANCIS R .	1855–	Born 6 June, 1821.
126.	COPE, THOMAS P.,	1829–1854.	{ Died 22 November, 1854, aged 85.
60.	COTTINEAU, DENNIS, . .	1801.	
49.	COX, PAUL. .	1799.	
51.	COXE, DANIEL WM . .	1800–1805.	{ Died 4 June, 1852, aged 88.
17.	CRAIG, JOHN, .	1793–1799.	Died May, 1807.
12.	CRAMOND, WILLIAM. . .	1792. 1795–1800.	Died 25 October, 1843.
41.	CRAWFORD, JAMES,	1797–1800.	

150. CUMMINGS, WILLIAM, . 1863–1867.
170. CUNNINGHAM, GRAHAM S., 1881.
155. CUSHMAN, CHARLES W., 1869–1880.

85. DALE, RICHARD, . . . 1803.   Died 24 Feb., 1826.
161. DAMON, ALBERT F., . . 1874–
143. DICKSON, JAMES N., . . 1851–1866.
87. DONATH, JOSEPH, . . . 1803–1819.
43. DONNALDSON, JOHN, . . 1798, 1799.   Died 29 Dec., 1831.
95. DOWNING, JACOB, . . . 1804.
115. DUNN, THOMAS, . . . 1810–1813.

34. EMERY, SAMUEL, . . . 1795–1797.
62. EMSLIE, ALEXANDER, . . 1801.   Died 1862, aged 91.
90. ENGLISH, THOMAS, . . 1803–1808.
61. EVANS, CADWALADER, . 1801.   Died 1841, aged 79.

163. FIELD, SAMUEL, 1874–1880, 1882–
44. FISHER, JAMES C., . 1798. 1800.
19. FITZSIMONS, THOMAS, 1794.   Died August, 1811.
22. FORDE, STANDISH, . . 1794–1797.
127. FOSTER, WILLIAM, . . 1829–1840.
37. FRANCIS, THOMAS W., 1796–1807.   { Died 2 June, 1815, aged 48.
25. FRY, JOHN, JR., . 1794–1796.

63. GARDINER, JOHN, JR., . 1801. 1803.
39. GOURDON, FERDINAND, . 1797.
156. GRISCOM, CLEMENT A., . 1870–

56. HAGA, GODFREY, . 1800–1825.   { Died 7 February, 1825, aged 78.
124. HARPER, CHARLES A., . 1826–1835.

92. HARRISON, GEORGE, .   1803.   Died 6 July, 1845.

146. HARRISON, GEORGE L.,   . 1854–

109. HARVEY, ISAAC, JR., .   1808–1810.   Died 1861, aged 90.

89. HARWOOD, ROBERT, . . 1803–1811.

50. HAWKINS, HENRY, . .   1800–1803.   { Died 16 November, 1815, aged 62.

48. HENRY, ALEXANDER, . .   1799–1847.   { Died 13 August, 1847, aged 82.

151. HENRY, T. CHARLTON,   1864–

74. HODGDON, SAMUEL, .   1802–1813.

26. HOLLINGSWORTH, JEHU. .   1794.   { Died May, 1819, aged 91.

139. HOSKINS, FRANCIS,   . . 1846–1857.

174. HOUSTON, HENRY H., . . 1884–

75. HUMPHREYS, ABEL, .   1802.

64. IMBERT, FELIX,   . . . 1801.

47. INGRAHAM, FRANCIS, . . 1799, 1800.

76. INSKEEP, JOHN, . . .   1802–1834.   { Died 18 December, 1834, aged 76. [Fourth president, 1 October, 1826 to 5 April, 1831.

176. JENKS, JOHN H., . . . 1885–

152. JESSUP, ALFRED D., . . 1866–1873.

104. JONES, SAMUEL W., . . 1807–1873.   { Born 11 Sept., 1781. Died 7 November, 1873, aged 92.

98. KEITH, SAMUEL, . . . 1805, 1806.   Died 4 April, 1852.

118. KRUMBHAAR, LEWIS, .   1812, 1813.

54. LARGE, EBENEZER, .   . 1800–1804.   Died November, 1810.

101. LARGE, JOHN, .   . 1806–1815.

108. LATIMER, THOMAS,   1808–1824.

13. LEAMY, JOHN, ... 1792–1806.

111. LEEDOM, RICHARD, . . 1809–1813.

113. LEIBERT, JOHN, . . 1809–1813.

173. LEWIS, ROBERT M., . . 1882–

29. McCALL, ARCHIBALD, 1794–1807. { Died 13 April, 1843, aged 75.

6. McCONNELL, MATTHEW, . 1792.

65. McCREA, JAMES, . . 1801.

166. McKEAN, THOMAS. . . 1877–

114. McKISSICK, JOHN, . . 1810–1813.

20. McMURTRIE, WILLIAM, . 1794, 1795. { Died 1 April, 1807, aged 69.

154. MADEIRA, LOUIS C., . . 1867–1880.

117. MARKOE, FRANCIS, . . 1812, 1813.

145. MASON, JOHN, . . . 1854–1874. { Died 1 September, 1874, aged 72.

77. MEEKER, SAMUEL, 1802, 1803.

96. MIFFLIN, SAMUEL, . . 1804–1809.

66. MIFFLIN, THOMAS, 1801, 1802. Died April, 1820.

83. MILLER, JOHN, JR., . 1803.

3. MILLER, MAGNUS, . . 1792–1799.

67. MILLIGAN, JAMES, . 1801.

9. MOORE, THOMAS L., 1792–1799. Died September, 1813.

7. MOYLAN, JASPER, . 1792. { Died 11 February, 1812, aged 53.

68. NAIRAC, PETER, . 1801.

135. NEFF, JOHN R., 1841–1863. { Died 24 July, 1863, aged 74.

5. NESBITT, JOHN M., . . 1792–1795. { Died 22 January, 1802, aged 74. First president, 11 December, 1792 to 13 January, 1796.

168. NEWBOLD, JOHN S., . . 1881–

30. Nicklin, Philip, . .	1794–1800.	Died Nov., 1806.
69. North, Joseph,	. 1801, 1802.	
46. Oldden, James,	. . 1798–1800.	
107. Palmer, John, .	. . 1808, 1809.	
84. Parker, Jeremiah, .	. . 1803.	
78. Pearce, Mathew,	. . 1802, 1803.	
120. Perry, Charles, . .	1817–1822.	
102. Pettit, Andrew, .	. 1806–1837.	Died 6 March, 1837.

8. Pettit, Charles, . . . 1792–1806.

{ Died 3 September, 1806, aged 69. Second president, 13 January, 1796 to 3 September, 1806. (Omit 9 January, 1798 to 8 July, 1799.)

158. Platt, Charles, . 1872–

Sixth president, 2 April, 1860. Vice-president and secretary, 13 Jan., 1863. Vice-president, 12 Jan., 1876. Seventh president, 14 Jan., 1878.

70. Poyntell, William, . .	1801. 1805–1811.	Died 10 Sept., 1811.
4. Prager, Michael,	. 1792, 1793.	Died 1793.
35. Pratt, Henry, .	1795.	{ Died 6 February, 1838, aged 76.
162. Price, Thomas C., .	1874–1881.	
16. Ralston, Robert,	. 1793–1799.	Died 11 August, 1836.
112. Ramsay, William,	. . 1809–1813.	
57. Read, James, .	. . 1800–1822.	
40. Read, William,	1797–1800.	
91. Rhoads, Samuel, . .	1803–1807.	
165. Rogers, Charles H, .	. 1877–1884.	Died 31 Dec., 1884.
10. Ross, John, . .	. 1792–1796.	
38. Rundle, Richard, . .	. 1796.	Died 26 May, 1826.
32. Sansom, William,	1795–1797.	
53. Simpson, John,	1800.	

105.	SMITH, EDWARD, . . .	1807–1857.	{ Died 7 June, 1859, aged 76.
129.	SMITH, JOHN C., . . .	1831–1845.	{ Died 22 June, 1845. Fifth president, 5 April, 1831 to 22 June, 1845.
24.	SMITH, ROBERT,	1794–1800.	
128.	SMITH, SAMUEL F., . .	{ 1830–1835. { 1838–1862.	{ Died 23 August, 1862, aged 84.
79.	SPERRY, JACOB, ...	1802, 1803.	
33.	STERETT, SAMUEL, .	1795–1798.	
11.	STEWART, WALTER, .	1792–1796.	
52.	STILLÉ, JOHN, .	{ 1800, 1803, 1804. { 1806–1840.	
80.	STOKES, WILLIAM, . . .	1802.	Died February, 1803.
14.	SWANWICK, JOHN, . . .	1792–1794.	
81.	TAGERT, JOSEPH, . .	1802–1813.	
132.	TAYLOR, CHARLES, .	1836–1873.	{ Died 14 January, 1874, aged 75.
88.	TAYLOR, JAMES,	1803–1808.	
134.	THOMAS, JACOB M.,	1840–1853.	{ Died October, 1853, aged 53.
28.	TINGEY, THOMAS, . .	1794.	
148.	TROTTER, EDWARD H.,	1858–1872.	{ Died 3 May, 1872, aged 58.
160.	TROTTER, WILLIAM H., .	1873–	
21.	VAUGHAN, JOHN, . .	1794–1798.	Died 30 Dec., 1841.
160.	WALN, JACOB S., .	1805–1824.	Died 4 April, 1850.
144.	WALN, S. MORRIS,	1852–1870	{ Died 21 December, 1870, aged 63.
82.	WALN, WILLIAM, .	1802.	{ Died February, 1826, aged 50.
71.	WARDER, JOHN, . . .	1801.	

122.	Weir, Silas E.,	1823–1828.	
167.	Welsh, John Lowber,	1879–	
137.	Welsh, William,	1842–1878.	{ Died 11 February, 1878, aged 70.
18.	West, Francis,	1793–1799.	Died 29 June, 1843.
94.	Wharton, Robert,	1804, 1805.	
164.	Wheeler, Charles,	1874–1883.	Died July, 1883.
133.	White, Ambrose,	1839–1873.	{ Died 29 December, 1873, aged 93.
124.	White, John,	1825–1848.	{ Died 14 February, 1848, aged 66.
153.	White, John P.,	1867, 1868.	
172.	Whitney, George,	1882–1885.	Died 6 March, 1885.
72.	Wikoff, Jacob C.,	1801–1831.	Died 23 May, 1834.
27.	Wilcocks, John,	1794.	
99.	Willing, Richard,	1805, 1806.	{ Died 18 June, 1858, aged 84.
159.	Winsor, Henry,	1873–	
136.	Wood, Richard D.,	1841–1869.	{ Died 6 April, 1869, aged 70.

Number of Directors Elected Annually.

Fifteen—1792, 1793. 1814–1845.

Twenty-five—1794–1813.

Nineteen—1852, 1853, 1877–1880.

Eighteen—1851, 1854–1857, 1866, 1867, 1869, 1870, 1872–1874.

Seventeen—1862–1865, 1868, 1871, 1875, 1876.

Sixteen—1846–1850. 1858–1861.

Twenty—1881–

TERMS OF DIRECTORS' SERVICE OVER TWENTY YEARS TO 1885.

Samuel W. Jones, ...	. 67 years.
Edward Smith, ...	. 51 "
Alexander Henry, ...	. 49 "
John A. Brown, ...	. 43 "
Thomas Astley, ...	. 40 "
John Stillé, ...	. 38 "
Charles Taylor, ...	. 38 "
William Welsh, ...	. 37 "
Arthur G. Coffin, ...	. 36 "
Ambrose White, ...	. 35 "
John Inskeep, ...	. 33 "
Andrew Pettit, ...	. 32
Jacob C. Wikoff, ...	. 32 "
George L. Harrison, ...	. 32 "—
Samuel F. Smith, ...	. 31 "
Francis R. Cope, ...	. 31 "—
Richard D. Wood, ...	. 29 "
Thomas P. Cope, ...	. 26 "
Edward S. Clarke, ...	. 24 "—
John White, ...	. 24
John R. Neff, ...	. 23 "
James Read, ...	. 23 "
John Mason, ...	. 21 "
Matthew L. Bevan, ...	. 20 "
Jacob S. Waln, ...	. 20 "
T. Charlton Henry, ...	. 22 "—

3.

LOCATION OF OFFICES.

Organized in Independence Hall, November, 1792.

Officers chosen, "City Tavern," 11 December, 1792.

I. 119 South Front street (now 213), 14 December, 1792–February, 1794.

II. Southeast corner of Walnut and Front streets, February, 1794–December, 1797.

III. Southwest corner of Walnut and Front streets, December, 1797–April, 1804.

IV. 98 South Second street (now 204), April, 1804–January, 1810.

V. 40 Walnut street (now 136), January, 1810–25 August, 1834.

VI. Walnut above Dock (now 216), 25 August, 1834–11 December, 1851.

VII. 60 Walnut street (now 232), 11 December, 1851.
56 and 58 Walnut street (now 228 and 230). The New Building embracing these three numbers was occupied 6 December, 1881.

MAIN OFFICE, LOOKING FROM THE HALL, OF THE INSURANCE COMPANY OF NORTH AMERICA.

4.

List of Original Stockholders of the Insurance Company of North America.

Adamson, Seth
Addison, Mathew
Ames, Dudley
Ames, John
Ames, Nathaniel
Anderson, Alexander
Andrews, Abraham
Andrews, Joseph
Appleton, Nathaniel, Jr.
Appleton, Nathaniel Walker
Ash, James
Ashton, George
Atkinson, John
Atwood, James
Austie, Thomas

Ball, Joseph
Ballantine, Thomas
Ballard, John
Balstead, J.
Barclay, John
Barnes, John
Barnes, Philip
Barnes, William
Barnet, Joseph

Bartleson, Abner
Barton, William
Barry, James
Beal, William
Beaman, Ephraim
Beates, Frederick
Beckford, William
Bell, Thomas
Bentley, Zach.
Biddiford, Preston
Biddle, William M.
Blanford, Charles
Blanford, William
Blodget, Samuel, Sen.
Blodget, Samuel, Jr.
Borland, John
Bourn, Shearjashub
Brackstone, Chandler
Bradford, James
Bradley, Charles
Brakstone, James
Bridges, Lawrence
Bringhurst, George
Broome, Hendreckson and
    Sumarl

Broome, Jacob
Brown, Philip
Bruce, Jonas
Brunson, Carter
Brunswick, Christopher
Buckley, Thomas
Burgess, William
Burrows, William W.
Burton, William
Butler, Hannah
Byrnes, Joseph

Cabot, Humphrey
Caldwell, John E.
Camberwell, Thomas
Cambridge, William
Campbell, David
Campbell, James
Campbell, William
Cane, Patrick
Cannada, Joseph
Carey, Joseph
Carnes, Adam
Carney, Peter
Carroll, David
Carter, Francis
Carter, George
Carter, Henry
Carter, J
Carter, James
Carter, John
Carter, Zebulon
Center, Charles
Chalmers, Samuel
Chaloner, John

Chester, John
Clark, John
Clarkson, George
Clarkson, Rebecca
Clarkson, William
Clessey, Myles F.
Coaster, Francis
Coddner, William
Codner, Joseph
Codwise, Charles
Coggeswell, Abraham
Colden, Christopher
Colhoune, Archibald
Collin, Joseph
Collins, James
Collins, John
Collins, Nathaniel
Collins, William
Colman, James
Colson, John
Comegys, Cornelius
Commyns, James
Commyns, William
Conner, Lewis
Conyngham, David H.
Conyngham, Nesbitt & Co.
Cooledge, Joseph
Cope, Joseph L.
Cordace, William
Correy, Mary
Correy, Robert
Corry, Israel
Colrain, James
Cotton, James
Cowderry, William

Coyle, John

Cox, Paul

Craig, John

Craigie, Robert

Cramond, William

Cranmore, Richard

Cranestown, Andrew

Crawford, James

Crawford, Peter

Creighton, J.

Cummings, Charles

Curwen, Joseph

Dale, Richard

Dallas, Alexander James

Dalling, Joseph

Dalton, George

Damer, Paul

Dana, Stephen

Danna, Richard

Davidson, Jonathan

Davidson, Joseph

Davidson, Peter

Davidson, Philemon

Davidson, William

Davis, Abner

Davis, Charles

Davis, J.

Davis, Leonard

Davis, William

Davison, Samuel

Dawson, Nicholas

Dean, Michael

Dearing, William

De Hart, Lewis

Delaforest, Antoine R. C. M.

Deunling, Frances Ch.

Dickenson, Philemon

Doughty, John

Douglas, Joseph

Duar, John

Dunbar, James

Duncan, Isaac

Duncan, Matthew

Dunlap, Samuel

Dunn, Arthur

Dunning, Joseph

Dunovan, John

Durnell, Thomas

Dwelling, Joseph

Dwight, Peter

Eddy, Peter

Ely, John

Erskine, Jonathan

Farmer, Thomas

Farrington, William

Field, Joseph

Fish, George

Fisk, R.

Fitzjames, James

Fitzpatrick, Donell

Fleischer, Balties

Flint, Jeremiah

Forman, Ezekiel

Forsythe, David

Fox, Edward

Francis, Tench

Franks, David S.

Frazer, Nicholas
Frazer, William
Frazier, Nalbro & John
Freemen, Jonathan
Freemen, Zebulon
Frobisher, William
Fry, John, Jr.
Furber, Thomas

Garrets, Peter
Gerrets, T.
Geyer, George
Gilford, Charles
Gill, Joseph Hewes
Gilman, Peter
Glentworth, James
Glentworth, Peter
Glover, Moses
Goodale, Richard
Goodnow, Peter
Gould, Henry
Granger, Jacob
Granger, Joseph
Green, Ashbel
Gregory, John

Hale, Thomas
Hall, J.
Hall, John
Hall, John K.
Hall, J. L.
Hall, Phillips
Hall, Thomas
Hamilton, George
Hamilton, Joseph

Hammatt, Benjamin
Harnis, James
Harrison, George
Hart, Ann
Hart, Solomon
Harthung, Jonathan
Harvey, Phillips
Hastings, Samuel
Hatch, Jabez T.
Haven, Nathan A.
Hawthorne, David
Hawthorne, James
Hawthorne, John
Haynes, Richard
Hays, Moses
Hazard, Ebenezer
Hemphill, William
Henderson, John
Henry, Alexander
Higgins, Francis
Higginson, Nathaniel C.
Hill, James
Hilton, Moses
Hodgson, A.
Hoffman, Jacob
Hoit, Lewis
Hollingsworth, Jehu, & Co.
Houston, John
Hunt, John
Hunt, Zacheies
Huntingdon, Jeremiah
Huntingdon, John
Hurst, Wenworth

Ingraham, Francis

Irwin, George
Irwin, John M.
Irwin, Matthew

Jackson, David
Jackson, J.
Jacobs, Moses
Jacobs, Samuel
James, George
James, Isaac
James, William
Jamieson, John
Jamieson, William
Jenkins, P.
Jenkins, Peter
Jenkins, Samuel
Jenkins, William Pitt
Jenks, Theodore
Jennys, Samuel
Johnsone, John
Joice, Andrew
Jones, Arthur
Jones, Charles
Jones, David
Jones, Isaac
Jones, John R.
Jones, Richard
Jones, Samuel
Jones S. P.
Jones, Sylvester
Jonstone, David

Kames, William
Kean, Peter
Keble, John

Kemble, Theophilus
Kendall, Thomas
Kendrick, James
Kenedy, Andrew
Kenedy, Samuel
Ketland, John
Ketland, Thomas, Jr.
Kidd, William
Kintzing, Abraham, Jr.
Kissick, John M.
Knogle, Abraham

Langdon, William
Larnard, Tristram
Laughton, James
Laughton, Richard
Lauman, George
Lawes, Robert
Lawrence, John
Leamy, John
Lee, William, Jr.
Lendall, Zachariah
Lewis, James Carter
Lewis, Samuel
Liman, Philemon
Lisle, John, Jr.
Livingtone, William G.
Loder, William
Lynch, Dominick

McAdam, Charles
McCall, Archibald, Jr.
McClenachan, Blair
McClintock, James
McClintock, Joseph

McConnell, Matthew
McCrea, James
McCree, John
McDonnaugh, Michael
McHenry, John
McHenry, James
McHenry, Walter
McIntyre, Andrew
McKenzie, Colin
McLane, William
McMullin, Samuel
McNeil, Daniel
McNeil, William
McQueen, Thomas
McRea, James
McWilliams, John
Mackey, Gershom
Macomb, John
Macon, Peter
Macpherson, William
Madison, Charles
Malborne, James
Mann, Abraham
Mansfield, George
Mansfield, William
Marsden, Moses
Marsden, William
Marston, David
Martin, J.
Martin, James
Mason, Andrew
Mason, James
Mason, Joseph
Mason, Noah
Mason, Paul

Mather, James
Mather, Timothy
Matlock, Joseph
Matthews, John
Maxwell, Leonard
Maynard, James
Maynard, Robert
Maynard, William
Meade, Robert
Means, John
Means, Peter
Means, Richard
Mecklin, Christopher C.
Mecklin, Philip
Mecklin, Thomas
Mecklinburg, Gerard
Medfield, Simon
Meeker, Cochran & Co.
Meleker, John
Melchior, Nehemiah
Melcher, Jacob
Melmooth, Philip
Mendez, Benjamin
Mendez, George
Mendez, Jonah
Merline, John
Merryman, William
Meserver, Paul
Meverick, Samuel
Meyer, Conrad
Miers, Henry
Miers, Moses
Miers, Richard
Miers, Samuel F.
Miers, Samuel J.

Miller, Magnus
Miller, Moses
Miller & Murray
Miller, William
Milligan, Catharine
Milligan, James
Milligan, Margaret
Milligan, Lewis
Milligan, Samuel
Mills, Sarah
Minor, Richard
Moore, Patrick
Moore, Thomas L.
Moreland, Francis
Morrill. J.
Morrill, Peter
Morris, William
Morton, Thomas
Moses, Solomon
Moylan, Jasper
Mulenbergen, Peter
Mulock, Edward
Mumford, James
Murray Alexander

Nelson, Samuel
Nesbitt, John Maxwell
Nilson, James
Nixon, John
Nunez, Benjamin
Nunez, Jacob

O'Donnell, Patrick
Oldden & Comegys
Oldden, James

Oliver, Peter
Otis, Samuel A.

Pain, James
Pain, George
Payson, George
Payton, Richard
Peirsol, Jeremiah
Pendleton, Samuel
Penrudoch, George
Perkins, Samuel
Perrin, William
Perry, Samuel
Pettit, Charles
Phelps, David
Phelps, Ebenezer
Phelps, James
Phelps, Samuel
Phillips, Alexander
Phlemer, Samuel
Pike, William
Potter, Richard
Prager, Mark, Jr.
Prager, Michael
Pragers & Co.
Pratt, Henry
Preston, Joseph
Preston, Philip
Preston, William
Prime, William
Porter, Andrew
Porter, Charles
Porter, James
Porter, Richard
Porter, Thomas

Pulsford, Alexander

Ralph, Micah
Ralston, Robert
Ramsay, John
Read, James
Read, William
Redwood, Charles
Redwood, John
Reid, James
Reinhart, Jacob
Rhea, Ebenezer
Richards, George
Richards, William, Jr.
Ritchie, Alexander
Rivington, J.
Rivington, Nathaniel
Roe, David
Rogers, Sarah
Rogers, William
Rogers, William G.
Ross, John
Ross, Joseph
Ross, R. H.
Russeller, Sarah
Rutgers, John

Sayers, James
Shaw, Thomas
Shoemaker, James
Simpson, George
Simpson, Sampson
Smith, Adam
Smith, John
Smith, Richard

Smith, William, South Carolina
Smith, William, 3d
Smith, William Moore
Smith, Y.
Smithson, Thomas
Smock, Robert
Small, Reuben
Snowden, Isaac, Jr.
Soams, Samuel
Springer, Samuel
Sproat, John
Stanley, Edward
Stamitz, P. K.
Stedley, Mary
Steel, Edward
Steele, Leonard
Steinmetz, John
Stewart, Archibald
Stewart, James
Stewart, Walter
Stickney, Thomas
Stimpson, Charles
Stimpson, Frederick
Stokes, Joseph
Stoodley, James
Storey, John, Jr.
Stoughton, John
Stuart, James, Jr.
Stuart, Rebecca R.
Summers, J.
Swanwick, John
Sykes, Peter

Taylor, John
Taylor, John M.

Taylor, Paul
Templeman, John
Thompson, Joseph
Thorp, Charles
Thorp, William
Tisdale, Lemuel
Todd, Eliphalet
Todd, John
Tracey, Richard
Treat, Robert
Turnbull, Charles
Turnbull, Walter

Van Dorp, Gerard
Vane, William
Vanhorn, William
Van Wyck, Abraham
Van Zandt, Guilian

Waite, John
Wallingford, Thomas
Walters, Timothy
Watson, John
Weed, Elijah
Weed, George
Weed, Mercer
Weed, William
Welch, Francis
Welch, Jacob
Welch, John
Welladvise, Moses
Wells, James
Wells, Peter
Welsh, Henry
Wendell, Thomas
10

Wentworth, Thomas
West, Francis and John
West, Zebulon
Wharton, Kearney
Wharton, Lloyd
Wheatly, Philip
Wheatly, Thomas
Wheaton, Gerard
Whitaker, James
Whitaker, Samuel
White, Abraham
White, Caleb
White, David
White, Henry
White, John
White, Jonathan
White, Nathaniel
White, Philemon
White, Philip
White, Samuel
Whiteford, Sampson
Wilkins, James
Wilks, Charles
Williams, Absolam
Williams, George
Williams, James
Williams, Lawrence
Williamson, James
Williamson, Jethro
Williamson, Nathaniel
Willington, James
Willington, Thomas
Willis, James
Willis, Joseph
Willis, Samuel

Wills, Isaac
Wills, Richard
Wills, Thomas
Wilmot, Simon
Wilmot, Christopher
Wilson, Charles
Wilson, Francis
Wilson, George
Wilson, James
Wilson, John
Wilson, T.
Wilson, Thomas
Wilson, W.
Wilson, William
Woods, Joseph

Woods, Michael
Wordley, James
Worthington, Charles
Woolf, Lewis
Wright, Charles
Wright, Christopher
Wright, J.
Wright, Stephen
Wrighton, Charles

Young, Charles
Young, Joseph

Zanting, Adam W.

5.

CHARTER AND SUPPLEMENTS.

AN ACT

TO INCORPORATE THE SUBSCRIBERS

TO THE

INSURANCE COMPANY OF NORTH AMERICA.

WHEREAS it is conceived that if a corporation, with a competent capital, and under proper regulations, were established, for the purpose of effecting insurances and transacting business connected therewith, advantages would result therefrom to the community in general, and to the mercantile interest in particular, by retaining in the State, as well the capital necessary for such a purpose, as also large sums of money which would otherwise be drawn from the country, for premiums and commissions to foreign correspondents, for effecting insurances, and also by more effectually securing the assured from the risques and dangers incident to the policies and assurances of private and particular persons: And whereas a number of the citizens of this commonwealth have by their petition to the legislature prayed that they may be incorporated for the purposes aforesaid:

SECTION 1. *Be it enacted by the Senate and House of Representatives of the Commonwealth of Pennsylvania, in General Assembly met, and it is hereby enacted by the authority of the same,* That the capital stock of the Insurance Company of North America shall amount to the sum of six hundred thousand dollars; that the same shall be divided into sixty thousand shares, of ten dollars each share, and the persons, co-partnerships, or bodies politic who have thereto subscribed, and have paid four dollars on each respective share, shall pay the residue of the sum and sums of

Capital stock of the Insurance Company of North America.

Number and amount of shares.

money due and payable for the share or shares by them respect-

ively subscribed, in the manner following, that is to say: two dollars on each share shall be paid on the second Monday of July, in the year one thousand seven hundred and ninety-four; two dollars on the second Monday of January, and two dollars on the second Monday of July, in the year one thousand seven

hundred and ninety-five. And any person or persons, co-part-nerships, or bodies politic, neglecting or refusing to pay all or any of the said several sums of money, at the time and times prescribed for payment thereof, shall respectively forfeit to the use of the company, all the monies previously paid on the account of the share and shares respectively, in payment whereof such default shall be made as aforesaid, together with all right, title, interest, emolument, profit, claim and demand, of, in, to and out of the funds of the said company, and the profits arising there-

from, by reason of such forfeited share and shares: And the funds of the said company shall, from time to time, be vested in securities for or evidences of debts due by the United States, or in the stock of the Bank of Pennsylvania, or of the Bank of the United States, or of the Bank of North America, or of the Schuylkill and Delaware Canal Company, or of the Schuylkill and Susquehanna Company, or of the Lancaster and Philadel-phia Turnpike Company, or of any other company that now is or hereafter may be incorporated by the State, in such manner, and in such sums, as the President and Directors of the said

company shall judge proper. *Provided always,* That all deposits for the safe keeping of the monies and securities of the said company shall be made respectively, in the Bank of Pennsylvania.

SECT. 2. *And be it further enacted by the authority aforesaid,* That the subscribers to the said company and their successors and assigns shall be, and they are hereby erected into a corporation, or body politic in law and in fact, under the name, style and title,

of "The President and Directors of the Insurance Company of North America"; and by the said name, style and title, shall have perpetual succession and all the powers, privileges and franchises, incident to a corporation; and shall be capable of taking, holding, and disposing of their said capital stock, and the

increase and profit thereof; and shall have full power and authority to make, have and use a common seal with such device and inscription as they shall deem proper, and the same to break, alter, and renew, at their pleasure; and by the name, style and title aforesaid, shall be able and capable in law to sue and be sued, plead and be impleaded, in any court or courts, before any Judge or Judges, Justice or Justices, in all manner of suits, pleas and demands whatsoever; and they are hereby authorized and empowered to make rules, bye-laws and ordinances, and to do every thing needful for the good government and support of the affairs of the said corporation: *Provided always,* That the said rules, bye-laws and ordinances, or any of them, shall not be repugnant to the Constitution and laws of the United States, and of this State.

Bye-laws not to be repugnant to the constitution and laws of the United States and this state.

SECT. 3. *And be it further enacted by the authority aforesaid,* That the said Corporation shall have a right and power to purchase, take, and hold real estate, and the same to demise, grant, sell, assign and convey, in fee simple, or otherwise: *Provided,* That the clear yearly income of the real estate to be held by the said Corporation, shall not, at any time exceed ten thousand dollars.

Power to hold real estate.

Limitation of the income thereof.

SECT. 4. *And be it further enacted by the authority aforesaid,* That for the well ordering the affairs of the said Corporation, there shall be twenty-five Directors (being Stockholders in the said company) chosen by ballot on the second Tuesday of January, in each and every year, by a plurality of the votes of the Stockholders present in person, or by proxy; and the Directors so chosen shall serve for one year next ensuing the elections respectively, and until others shall be chosen, and no longer; and at their first meeting after each election shall choose one of their number as President: *Provided always nevertheless,* That John Maxwell Nesbitt, shall be the present President, and Joseph Ball, John Craig, John Leamy, John Swanwick, Walter Stewart, Samuel Blodget, the younger, Magnus Miller, Thomas Fitzsimons, William M'Murtrie, John Vaughan, Charles Pettit, John Ross, Robert Ralston, Francis West, Standish Ford, Peter Blight, Thomas Lloyd Moore, Robert Smith, John Fry, the younger, John Hollingsworth, John Wilcox, Thomas Tingey, Archibald M'Call, and Philip Nicklin, shall be the present Directors, and shall continue in office until the second Tuesday in January next; *Provided also,* That in case it shall at any time happen that an election of Directors shall not be made upon any day, when, pursuant to this act, it ought to have been made the said corporation shall not for that cause be deemed to be dissolved, but it shall be lawful on any other day, within ten days thereafter, to hold and make an election of Directors, in such manner as shall have been regulated by the bye-laws and ordinances of the said Corporation; and that in case of the death, resignation, or absence from the State, of a Director, or in case any Director shall be chosen a Director of any other Insurance Company, and shall act as such, the place of such Director shall be filled up by a new choice for the remainder of the year, in manner aforesaid, at such time and place as shall be appointed by the Board of

Of the election of Directors.

Their time of service.

Of the President.

Present Directors.

Election not made on the charter day, no dissolution of the corporation.

Of vacancies in the office of Directors.

Directors, twenty days notice of such election having been given in two of the public newspapers of the City of Philadelphia.

Sect. 5. *And be it further enacted by the authority aforesaid,* That the said Company shall be obliged by force and virtue of this act, from time to time, to cause such a stock of ready money to be provided and reserved, as shall be sufficient to answer all just demands upon their policies of insurance, for any losses which shall happen, and shall ratify, pay and discharge all such demands, according to the tenor and effect of such policies of insurance; and in case of refusal or neglect to pay such losses, after thirty days notice thereof, the stock and effects of the said Company shall be liable to the party injured, upon judgment and execution obtained.

Of the ready money stock of the Corporation.

Of payment of losses.

Stock and effects liable, on judgment and execution.

Sect. 6. *And be it further enacted by the authority aforesaid,* That the Directors for the time being shall have power to appoint such officers, clerks and servants, under them, as shall be necessary for executing the business of the said Corporation, and to allow them such compensation for their services, respectively, as shall be reasonable; and shall be capable of exercising such other powers and authorities, for the well governing and ordering of the affairs of the said Corporation, as shall be described, fixed and determined by the laws, regulations and ordinances of the same.

Of the appointment and compensations of the officers of the Corporation.

Sect. 7. *And be it further enacted by the authority aforesaid,* That the following rules, restrictions, limitations and provisions, shall form and be fundamental articles of the Constitution of said Corporation, to wit:

Fundamental rules.

First, The Stockholders shall be entitled, on all questions coming before them, to one vote for each share of the stock by them respectively held, to the number of fifty shares; and for every ten shares above fifty, one vote; but no Stockholder, either in his own right, or as proxy, shall have more than one hundred votes; nor shall any Stockholder vote at any election for Directors, unless the stock shall have stood in his or her name in the books of the Company, at least three months preceding the time of such election. All Stockholders may vote in elections, or on any question touching the business of the Corporation, by proxy; provided the proxy be derived directly from such Stockholders, and the vote be given by a citizen of this Commonwealth.

Of voting by the stockholders.

Second, No Director shall be entitled to any emolument, unless the same shall have been allowed by the Stockholders, at a

Of compensation to the Directors.

general meeting; but the Stockholders shall make such compensation to the President, for his extraordinary attendance on the business of the Corporation, as shall appear to them reasonable. *And President.*

Third, The Directors shall divide themselves into committees, each committee to consist of three Directors; and the committees shall attend, in a weekly rotation, at the office of the company, and, together with the President, shall have full power and authority, in the name and on behalf of the Corporation, to make such insurances upon vessels and merchandise at sea, or going to sea, or upon any goods, wares or merchandise, or other personal property, going or gone by land or water, or in dwelling-houses, ware-houses or stores, or upon buildings, against the risque arising from fire, or upon the life or lives of any person or persons, and to lend money upon bottomry and respondentia, and, generally, to transact and perform all the business relating to the objects aforesaid; but the said committees shall always act in conformity to such regulations as the Stockholders shall make, and subject to the orders and instructions of the Board of Directors. *Of the weekly committees of Directors. Their power to insure and lend money, and on what objects; Subject to the regulations and orders of the Board of Directors.*

Fourth, There shall be stated meetings of the Board of Directors, at least once a fortnight and occasional meetings at such other times, as the President shall think proper. The President shall preside at all meetings of the Corporation, but he shall have no vote (except in cases of election) unless there is an equality of votes, when he shall decide the question. In case of the sickness or the necessary absence of the President, his place may be supplied by any other Director, whom the Board of Directors, shall for that purpose appoint. Seven of the Directors, (whereof the President shall always be one) shall form a quorum of the Board of Directors; but in the absence of the President, a majority of the whole number of Directors shall be requisite to form a quorum. And all questions before the Board shall be decided by a plurality of votes, but no vote shall be reconsidered by a smaller number of Directors than was present when such vote was passed. *Of meetings of the Board of Directors. In what case the President may vote. How his absence shall be supplied. Of a quorum of the Board. Of the decision of all questions by the Board.*

Fifth, A number of Stockholders, who, together, shall be proprietors of not less than six thousand shares, or upwards, shall have power at any time to call a general meeting of the Stockholders, for purposes relative to the institution, giving at least six weeks notice in two public gazettes of the City of Philadelphia, and specifying in such notice the object or objects of such meeting. *Of calling a general meeting of the Stockholders.*

Sixth, The Corporation shall not, directly or indirectly, engage in the business of banking, nor deal nor trade in any thing except the objects herein before specified, bills of exchange, gold or silver bullion, or in the sale of goods really and truly pledged for premiums due and not paid, or of goods, which shall be the produce of its lands.

Restrictions on the trading of the Corporation.

Seventh, The stock of the said Corporation shall be assignable and transferable, according to such rules as shall be instituted in that behalf by the laws and ordinances of the same.

Of transfers of the stock.

Eighth, The Directors shall, on the second Monday of January, and on the second Monday of July, in each and every year, declare a dividend of so much of the profits of the Corporation as to them shall appear advisable, and the dividend so declared shall be paid to the respective proprietors in ten days after the same shall be made, but the monies received as premiums on risques, which shall be undetermined and outstanding at the time of making such dividend, shall not be considered as a part of the profits of the Corporation; and in case of any loss or losses whereby the capital stock of the Company shall be lessened, no subsequent dividend shall be made until a sum equal to such diminution, and arising from the profits of the Corporation, shall have been added to the capital.

Of dividends.

Ninth, Any member of the Corporation may nevertheless become assured thereby on any vessel, goods, wares, merchandise, or lives, in the same manner, and with the same effect, as if such member had no interest in the Corporation.

Members of the Corporation may be insured.

Tenth, The Directors shall keep fair and regular entries in a book or books (for that purpose to be provided) of their proceedings, and submit the same, if required, to the inspection of the Stockholders at every of their stated meetings.

Of the books to be kept by the Directors.

Eleventh, A book, containing the names of the Stockholders, shall be kept, and shall at all reasonable times be open to any Stockholder requiring the same.

Of a book containing the names of the stockholders.

SECT. 8. *And be it further enacted by the authority aforesaid*, That if the said Corporation, or any person or persons for or to the use of the same, shall engage in the business of banking, or deal or trade in buying or selling any goods, wares, merchandise or commodities whatsoever, contrary to the provisions of this act, all and every person or persons, who shall have given any order or direction for so engaging, dealing and trading, and all and every

Penalty, in case of trading contrary to this act.

person and persons, who shall have been concerned, as parties or agents therein, shall forfeit and lose treble the value of the monies discounted, and of the goods, wares, merchandise and commodities traded or dealt in, one-half thereof to the use of the informer, and the other half to the use of the State, to be recovered with costs of suit.

SECT. 9. *And be it further enacted by the authority aforesaid,* That this act shall be and continue in force until the first day of January, which will be in the year of our Lord one thousand eight hundred and fifteen: *Provided always,* That for the liquidation and settlement of all the past transactions and accounts of the said company, the corporate powers thereof shall be and continue effectual to all intents and purposes: *And provided also,* That nothing in this act shall be taken or construed to affect the rights of any person, persons or bodies politic before the passing of this act.

Limitation of the charter to the first of January, 1815.

GEORGE LATIMER, *Speaker*
Of the House of Representatives.

ANTHONY MORRIS, *Speaker*
Of the Senate.

Approved, the fourteenth of April, 1794.

THOMAS MIFFLIN, *Governor*
Of the Commonwealth of Pennsylvania.

A SUPPLEMENT

To the Act entitled "An Act to Incorporate the Subscribers to the Insurance Company of North America."

SECTION 1. *Be it enacted by the Senate and House of Representatives of the Commonwealth of Pennsylvania, in General Assembly met, and it is hereby enacted by the authority of the same,* That from and after the passing of this act, the funds of the said company may from time to time be vested in securities for, or evidence of debts due by the United States, or in the stock of any Bank or other institution, which is or may be incorporated in the State of Pennsylvania, in their own stock, or in bills of exchange, or may

The funds may be vested in evidence of debt of United States or bank stock, &c.

be loaned to the State of Pennsylvania, or on the security of real estate within the same.

SECT. 2. *And be it further enacted by the authority aforesaid,* That for the well ordering the affairs of the said corporation there shall hereafter be fifteen Directors (stockholders in said company) chosen by ballot, on the second Tuesday of January, annually, by a plurality of votes of the stockholders, present or by proxy. And the Directors so chosen shall serve for one year next ensuing the elections, respectively and until others shall be chosen, and no longer; and at their first meeting after each election shall choose one of their number President; and in case of the death, resignation, or absence from the State (six months at one time) of a Director, or in case any Director shall cease to be a stockholder, or be chosen a Director of any other Insurance Company and shall act as such, the place of such Director may be filled by a new choice for the remainder of the year, by a majority of the Board of Directors.

Fifteen Directors to be chosen.

Term of service.

How vacancies to be filled.

SECT. 3. *And be it further enacted by the authority aforesaid,* That five Directors, whereof the President to be one, shall form a quorum of the Board of Directors; but in the absence of the President, a majority of the whole number of Directors shall be requisite to form a quorum.

How many Directors to form a quorum.

SECT. 4. *And be it further enacted by the authority aforesaid,* That no stockholder indebted to the said company shall be permitted to make a transfer of his stock, or receive a dividend thereon until such debt is discharged, or satisfactory security be given to the Board of Directors for the same.

No transfer to be made or dividend received by a stockholder untill his debts are paid or secured.

SECT. 5. *And be it further enacted by the authority aforesaid,* That the charter of the said Insurance Company of North America, as altered and amended by this supplement, be, and the same is hereby extended and continued in full force, until the first day of January, which will be in the year of our Lord, one thousand eight hundred and thirty-five, with all the powers, provisions and restrictions, contained in the said original charter; excepting only, that so much of the act to which this is a supplement, as is hereby altered and supplied, and no more, be and the same is hereby repealed: *Provided always,* That after the said first day of January, one thousand eight hundred and thirty-five, the corporate powers of the said company shall remain and continue for the liquidation and settlement of their past transactions and for no other purpose whatsoever: *And provided also,* That if it shall appear that the charter and privileges hereby

Charter extended until 1835.

Proviso for liquidation of accounts.

Proviso for annulling the charter.

renewed and granted are injurious to the citizens of this commonwealth, the Legislature shall have full power to revoke and cancel them at any time they may think proper.

JOHN TOD, *Speaker*
Of the House of Representatives.

P. C. LANE, *Speaker*
Of the Senate.

Approved the twenty-eighth day of January, one thousand eight hundred and thirteen.

SIMON SNYDER.

EXTRACT

From An Act to incorporate the "Chambersburg Insurance Company," &c.

SECTION 1. *Be it enacted by the Senate and House of Representatives of the Commonwealth of Pennsylvania, in General Assembly met, and it is hereby enacted by authority of the same,* That an act entitled "An Act to Incorporate the subscribers to the Insurance Company of North America," passed the fourteenth day of April, seventeen hundred and ninety-four, and the supplement thereto, entitled "a supplement to the act entitled an act to incorporate the subscribers to the Insurance Company of North America," passed the twenty-eighth day of January, one thousand eight hundred and thirteen, be and the same are hereby continued in full force and virtue for the term of twenty years from and after the first day of January, one thousand eight hundred and thirty-five.

Charters extended twenty years from first of January, 1835.

SECT. 35. *And be it further enacted by the authority aforesaid,* That the Legislature reserve the right to revoke or alter the charters extended or granted by this act in any way that may be deemed conducive to the interests of the State.

SAM'L ANDERSON, *Speaker*
Of the House of Representatives.

JESSE R. BURDEN, *Speaker*
Of the Senate.

Approved the third day of April, A. D. one thousand eight hundred and thirty-three.

GEORGE WOLF.

EXTRACT

From an Act to incorporate the Washington Insurance Company of Philadelphia, and for other purposes.

Additional privileges granted. SECT. 20. In addition to the privileges heretofore granted it shall and may be lawful for the Insurance Company of North America to invest their capital stock and other funds in the public stocks or loans of any of the United States or of any city, company, or institution, now or that hereafter may be incorporated by the United States or any individual State, or in ground rents, mortgages, or other good and sufficient securities in this State, and the said investment from time to time to alter, change, and renew, as the interests or circumstances of the Company may render expedient.

LEWIS DEWART, *Speaker*
Of the House of Representatives.

CHARLES B. PENROSE, *Speaker*
Of the Senate.

Approved the tenth day of April, one thousand eight hundred and thirty-eight.

JOSEPH RITNER.

A FURTHER SUPPLEMENT

To the Act entitled "An Act to Incorporate the Subscribers to the Insurance Company of North America," and the Supplements thereto.

Charter perpetual.

Legislature may annul. SECTION 1. *Be it enacted by the Senate and House of Representatives of the Commonwealth of Pennsylvania, in General Assembly met, and it is hereby enacted by the authority of the same:* That the Charter of the President and Directors of the "Insurance Company of North America" shall be perpetual; subject, nevertheless, to the right of the Legislature to alter, annul, or repeal the same whenever it may be deemed conducive to the interests of the State.

WM. HOPKINS, *Speaker*
Of the House of Representatives.

CHARLES B. PENROSE, *Speaker*
Of the Senate.

Approved the eleventh day of October, eighteen hundred and thirty-nine.

DAVID R. PORTER.

A FURTHER SUPPLEMENT

To the Act entitled "An Act to Incorporate the Subscribers to the Insurance Company of North America."

WHEREAS, The President and Directors of the Insurance Company of North America, have made request that they may be permitted to reduce the amount of their capital; Therefore,

SECTION 1. *Be it enacted by the Senate and House of Representatives of the Commonwealth of Pennsylvania, in General Assembly met, and it is hereby enacted by the authority of the same,* That it shall be lawful for the said Insurance Company, whenever a majority in number and value of the Stockholders shall deem it expedient and express their assent thereto in writing, to reduce the capital stock of the said Company to the sum of three hundred thousand dollars, and the par value of the shares of the said stock to five dollars each, and if at any time it shall be ascertained that the assets of the Company exceed the said sum of three hundred thousand dollars, such excess shall be divided among the Stockholders in proper proportion, according to the number of their shares, in such manner and at such times as shall be deemed by the Directors consistent with a proper attention to the judicious collection and conversion of the assets, and the prudent management of the business of the Company.

Capital North American Insurance Company reduced.

SECT. 2. That such assent in writing may be signed by the Stockholders or their attorneys duly constituted, and may be recorded in the office for recording deeds, in the city and county of Philadelphia, and a certified copy or exemplification of such record shall in all cases be received in evidence, and be as valid and effectual as the original instrument.

Assent of Stockholders.

SECT. 3. That when such assent in writing shall be given and expressed as aforesaid, the capital stock of the Company and the par value of the shares, shall be thenceforth reduced in the manner and to the sums mentioned in the first section of this act, and notice thereof shall be given by advertisements for four weeks in two at least of the daily newspapers of the city of Philadelphia: *Provided nevertheless,* That the whole of the amount of the capital stock of the said Company existing at the date of the said advertisements, shall be liable for contracts of insurance existing with said Company at that time.

Public notice to be given of reduction.

SECT. 4. That the President of the said Company shall, upon a vote of the Board of Directors to that effect, or on the application of a number of Stockholders, who together shall be proprietors of six thousand shares, call a general meeting of the Stockholders, giving at least two weeks' notice in two of the daily papers of the City of Philadelphia, and specifying in such notice the object or objects of such meeting.

SECT. 5. That deposites, for the safe keeping of the moneys and securities of the said Company, may be made in any of the incorporated banks in the city and county of Philadelphia.

SECT. 6. That so much of any act relating to the said Company as is hereby altered or supplied, be, and the same is hereby repealed.

SECT. 7. That no person shall be allowed to vote by proxy at any election of said Corporation, and no stock which is hypothecated, shall entitle the holder thereof to vote at any such elections.

JAMES ROSS SNOWDEN, *Speaker*
Of the House of Representatives.

JOHN STROHM, *Speaker*
Of the Senate.

Approved the sixth day of April, one thousand eight hundred and forty-two.

DAVID R. PORTER.

A FURTHER SUPPLEMENT

To the Act entitled "An Act to Incorporate the Insurance Company of North America."

SECTION 1. *Be it enacted by the Senate and House of Representatives of the Commonwealth of Pennsylvania, in General Assembly met, and it is hereby enacted by the authority of the same,* That the Insurance Company of North America be, and they are hereby authorized to increase the number of Directors of the said Company to twenty.

FINDLEY PATTERSON, *Speaker*
Of the House of Representatives.

WILLIAM P. WILCOX, *Speaker*
Of the Senate.

Approved the eleventh day of February, one thousand eight hundred and forty-five.

FRS. R. SHUNK.

A FURTHER SUPPLEMENT

To the Act entitled "An Act to Incorporate the Subscribers to the Insurance Company of North America."

WHEREAS the President and Directors of the Insurance Company of North America, are desirous to be permitted to increase their capital stock, and restore the par value of the shares of their stock to the original amount and value. Therefore,

SECTION 1. *Be it enacted by the Senate and House of Representatives of the Commonwealth of Pennsylvania, in General Assembly met, and it is hereby enacted by the authority of the same,* That it shall be lawful for the said Insurance Company of North America, whenever a majority of the Stockholders, at any meeting regularly convened, shall deem it expedient, and express their assent thereto, to increase the capital stock of the said Company to the sum of five hundred thousand dollars, and the par value of the shares of said stock to ten dollars each: *Provided,* That the amount of the effective funds of the said Company, shall be equal to five hundred thousand dollars beyond reservations and claims for existing business, and be invested and set apart as their capital.

Increase of capital stock to $500,000, and par value of shares $10.

SECT. 2. That so much of any act relating to the said Company as is hereby affected, altered, or supplied, be, and the same is hereby repealed.

J. S. McCALMONT, *Speaker*
Of the House of Representatives.

V. BEST, *Speaker*
Of the Senate.

Approved the eighth day of May, one thousand eight hundred and fifty.

WM. F. JOHNSTON.

A FURTHER SUPPLEMENT

To the Act entitled "An Act to Incorporate the Subscribers to the Insurance Company of North America."

SECTION 1. *Be it enacted by the Senate and House of Representatives of the Commonwealth of Pennsylvania, in General Assembly met, and it is hereby enacted by the authority of the same,* That the President and Directors of the Insurance Company of North America be, and they are hereby authorized and empowered to appoint agents or officers to effect insurances in any of the other States of the Union, or without its limits, and that contracts of insurance effected by such agents or officers, shall be as valid and binding as if the same were effected by the President and Directors aforesaid, in the State of Pennsylvania, and the said Insurance Company of North America shall have all the other powers and privileges conferred on or exercised by the Union Mutual and Delaware Mutual Safety Insurance Companies, of Philadelphia.

E. B. CHASE, *Speaker*
Of the House of Representatives.

M. McCASLIN, *Speaker*
Of the Senate.

Approved the twenty-seventh day of February, one thousand eight hundred and fifty-four.

WM. BIGLER.

A FURTHER SUPPLEMENT

To an Act entitled "An Act to Incorporate the Subscribers to the Insurance Company of North America."

SECTION 1. *Be it enacted by the Senate and House of Representatives of the Commonwealth of Pennsylvania, in General Assembly met, and it is hereby enacted by the authority of the same,* That it shall be lawful for the said Insurance Company of North America, whenever a majority of the Stockholders at any meeting regularly convened shall deem it expedient and express their assent thereto, to increase the capital stock of the said Company to the sum of one million dollars; the par value of the shares of the said stock to twenty (20) dollars: *Provided,* That the said amount of one million dollars beyond reservations and claims for existing business shall be invested and set apart as the capital of the Company.

SECT. 2. That the stated meetings of the Board of Directors shall be held once every month, and occasional meetings at such other times as the President shall think proper.

SECT. 3. The officers of the Company, or any of them, when authorized by the Board of Directors, shall have full power and authority in the name and on behalf of the Corporation, to make all kinds of marine insurance, all kinds of insurance by inland transportation, all kinds of insurance against fire, in city, town and country, upon the life or lives of any person or persons, and to lend money upon bottomry and respondentia, and generally to transact and perform all the business relating to the objects aforesaid, but the said officers shall always act in conformity to such regulations as the Directors may prescribe.

SECT. 4. That so much of any Act relating to the said Company as is hereby affected, altered or supplied, be and the same is hereby repealed.

JAMES H. WEBB, *Speaker*
Of the House of Representatives.

WILLIAM H. WALLACE, *Speaker*
Of the Senate.

Approved the fourteenth day of March, Anno Domini one thousand eight hundred and seventy-one.

JNO. W. GEARY.

EXTRACT

From an Act entitled "A Supplement to an Act entitled 'An Act to Establish an "Insurance Department,' approved the fourth day of April, one thousand "eight hundred and seventy-three, providing for the incorporation and regu- "lation of Insurance Companies, and relating to Insurance Agents and Brokers "and to Foreign Insurance Companies."

SECTION 27. Any existing fire or fire and marine insurance company, and any stock company formed under this act, may at any time increase the amount of its capital stock, if authorized so to do by the stockholders holding the larger amount in value of the stock, at a meeting specially called for that purpose, of which at least sixty days' previous public notice shall have been given. At such meeting of the stockholders and at all other meetings thereof, each stockholder shall be entitled to cast either in person or by proxy, subject to such regulations, as to voting by proxy, as the by-laws of the company may prescribe, one vote for each share of stock that shall have stood in his or her name on the books of the company for at least three months previous thereto, increase of capital stock as aforesaid may be made by increasing the number of the shares of stock or by increasing the par value of the same, and such increased shares or increased par value shall be allotted *pro rata* to the stockholders of said company according to their interest, and may be paid *in* whole or in part out of the accumulated reserve of the company in case the condition of the company warrants such allotments, or the same may be disposed of as is provided in this act for the organization of stock companies. No portion of the funds of a company shall be regarded as accumulated reserve subject to allotment under this section, except such amounts as may remain after charging the entire amount of premium receipts on undetermined policies in addition to capital stock and all other liabilities, before any such company as aforesaid shall be authorized to increase its capital stock as herein provided, it shall file with the Insurance Commissioner a certificate setting forth the amount and manner of such desired increase and the proceedings of the stockholders authorizing the same, and thereafter such company shall be entitled to have the increased amount of capital fixed by said certificate, and the examination of securities composing the capital stock thus increased shall be made in the same manner as is provided in this act for capital stock originally paid in. Whenever any existing fire or fire and marine insurance company shall, by a resolution of its board of directors, accept of the provisions of this section of this act as a part of the charter of the said company, and a duly certified copy of such resolution shall have been filed in the office of the Insurance Commissioner, the charter of said company shall be deemed and taken to have been amended by the addition thereto of this section, which shall have the same force and effect as if a part of the company's original charter or constituting a supplement thereto.

SAMUEL F. PATTERSON, *Speaker*
Of the House of Representatives.

JOHN LATTA, *President*
Of the Senate.

Approved the first day of May, Anno Domini one thousand eight hundred and seventy-six.

J. F. HARTRANFT.

Approved and adopted by the stockholders at a meeting held the tenth day of July, one thousand eight hundred and seventy-six.

MATTHIAS MARIS,
Secretary.

6.

MARINE BUSINESS BY DECADES.

	PREMIUMS.	LOSSES.
15 December, 1792, 31 December, 1802,	$6,037,456 71	$5,500,887 57
1 January, 1803, 31 December, 1812,	1,364,637 48	1,583,836 47
1 January, 1813, 31 December, 1822,	276,764 30	335,554 06
1 January, 1823, 31 December, 1832,	160,138 70	227,954 57
1 January, 1833, 31 December, 1842,	428,584 16	358,332 78
1 January, 1843, 31 December, 1852,	2,855,189 98	2,153,679 96
1 January, 1853, 31 December, 1862,	3,102,440 79	2,866,197 28
1 January, 1863, 31 December, 1872,	6,082,496 86	4,582,561 37
1 January, 1873, 31 December, 1882,	16,862,964 89	14,281,263 72
	$37,170,673 87	$31,890,267 78
1883 and 1884,	3,032,960 49	2,012,928 49
	$40,203,634 36	$33,903,196 27

7.

Fire Business by Decades.

—

	PREMIUMS.	LOSSES.
15 December, 1794, } 31 December, 1802, }	$81,253 76	$30,116 59
1 January, 1803, } 31 December, 1812, }	98,647 95	23,873 30
1 January, 1813, } 31 December, 1822, }	69,224 20	1,569 44
1 January, 1823, } 31 December, 1832, }	61,639 33	17,973 87
1 January, 1833, } 31 December, 1842, }	114,326 34	78,948 27
1 January, 1843, } 31 December, 1852, }	554,267 08	382,407 43
1 January, 1853, } 31 December, 1862, }	1,138,164 24	424,448 32
1 January, 1863, } 31 December, 1872, }	8,687,020 03	5,193,242 87
1 January, 1873, } 31 December, 1882, }	15,516,731 90	8,701,920 24
	$26,321,274 83	$14,854,500 33
1883 and 1884.	4,482,661 29	2,768,244 74
	$30,803,936 12	$17,622,745 07

8.

LIST OF EARLY PHILADELPHIA UNDERWRITERS.

Names of some of the early Philadelphia Underwriters on Policies issued from the offices of Joseph Saunders, Thomas Wharton, Walter Shee, and Kidd & Bradford.

I am indebted to Mr. C. R. Hildeburn for many of these policies. Those of Kidd & Bradford's clients are derived from their books as enumerated in Mr. Wallace's *Table of Contents* of Colonel Bradford's papers in possession of the Historical Society of Pennsylvania, *Philadelphia,* 1878.

Aspden, Mathias

Bache, Theophylact and Richard
Baynton, John
Baynton & Wharton
Bell, John
Benezet, Philip
Beveridge, David
Bright & Bechin
Bringhurst, ———
Bryan, George

Caldwell, Andrew
Chalmers, James
Chevalier, John and Peter
Child & Stiles
Clark, Daniel
Conyngham & Nesbitt
Cox, Isaac

Coxe, William

Davis, William

Emlen, George, Jr.
Emlen, George & Caleb
Emlen & Warder
Evans, William

Francis, Tench
Francis & Relfe
Franks, David

Harrison, Henry
Harvey, William
Hicks, Augustus, 1749.
Hodge & Bayard
Howell, Samuel, & Son
Hughes, John

James & Drinker

Jones, Aquilla

Jones, Charles

Judah, Abraham

Kelly, William

Lightfoot, Thomas & William

Levy, Isaac

McCall, Archibald, 1749.

McCall, Samuel, 1749.

McClanachan, Blair

McMurtrie, David

McMurtrie, William, & Co.

Mease, John

Mease, Mathew

Mease & Caldwell

Meredith, Reese

Mifflin, John, 1749.

Mifflin & Massey

Mifflin, Samuel

Moore, Philip

Moore, William

Morris, Robert

Morton, John

Nesbitt, John M.

Nixon, John

Oldman, Samuel

Pemberton & Edwards

Pringle, John

Purviance, Samuel

Reed & Pettit

Riché, Thomas

Robinson & Reynolds

Ross, John

Rundle, Daniel

Scott & McMichael

Shee, John

Smith, George

Stedman, Charles, & Co.

Stocker, Anthony

Strettell, Amos

Warder, Jeremiah

White, Townsend

Wilcocks, John

Willing, Morris & Co.

Willing, Thomas, and Company

Yorke, Dennis

Yorke, Thomas

John Alsop and James Jauncey, of New York, also underwrote in Kidd & Bradford's office.

One of Joseph Saunders' policies of 1749 follows; the written portion is given in SMALL CAPITALS. The endorsement (also written) gives the record in Mr. Saunders' book, *vide* p. 17.

9

A Philadelphia Marine Policy of 1749.

In the name of GOD, *Amen*, I John Kidd of the City of *Philadelphia*, Merchant have made Assurance, and cause to be assured (Lost or not Lost) at and from the Port of Philadelphia to London upon all kind of lawful Goods, Cash or Merchandize, laden or to be laden upon the good Ship called the Griffin of the Burthen of Tons, or thereabouts, whereof is Master under GOD, for this present voyage Joseph Arthur or whosoever else shall go for Master in the said Ship, or by whatsoever other Name or Names the same Ship, or the Master thereof, is, or shall be named or called, beginning the Adventure upon the said lawful Goods or Merchandize, at and from the Port of Philadelphia aforesaid and so shall continue and endure until the said Goods and Merchandizes shall be safely landed at London aforesaid. And it shall and may be lawful for the said Ship, in her Voyage, to proceed and sail to, touch and stay at any Ports or Places, if thereunto obliged by stress of Weather, or other unavoidable Accident, without Prejudice to this Insurance. Touching the Adventures and Perils, which we the Assurers are contented to bear, and do take upon us in this Voyage, they are, of the *Seas, Men of War, Fires, Enemies, Pirates, Rovers, Thieves, Jettesons, Letters of Mart and Counter Mart, Surprisals, Taking at Sea, Arrests, Restraints and Detainments of all Kings, Princes or People of what Nation, Condition or Quality soever, Baratry of the Master and Mariners*, and all other Perils, Losses, and Misfortunes, that have or shall come to the Hurt, Detriment or Damage of the said Goods or Merchandize or to any Part thereof. And in case of any Losses or Misfortunes, it shall be lawful to and for the Assured Factors, Servants and Assigns, to sue, labour and travel for, in and about the Defence, Safeguard and Recovery of the said Goods and Merchandize, or any Part thereof, without Prejudice to this Insurance; to the Charges whereof we the Assurers will contribute each one, according to the Rate and Quantity of his sum herein assured. And it is agreed by us the Assurers that this Writing or Policy of Assurance, shall be of as much Force and Effect, as the surest Writing or Policy of Assurance heretofore made in *Lombard-Street*, or elsewhere in *LONDON*, and so we the assurers are contented, and do hereby promise and bind ourselves each one for his own Part, our Heirs, Executors and Goods, to the Assured THEIR Executors, Administrators and Assigns, for the true Performance of the Premisses, confessing ourselves paid the Consideration due unto us for this Assurance, by the said Assured or HIS Assigns, at FOUR ₱ CENT.

In Witness Whereof, WE the Assurers have subscribed our Names and sums Assured in *Philadelphia*, the TWENTY-FIFTH Day of APRIL, one Thousand Seven Hundred and Forty-NINE.

Memorandum. *It is agreed by and between the Assured and Assurers, that in Case of any Loss above Five per Cent., there shall be no Abatement. But that in Case of any Average Loss not exceeding Five Pounds per Cent., the Assurers, by Agreement, are not to pay or allow any Thing towards such Loss.*

It is further agreed, That if any Dispute shall arise, relating to a Loss on this POLICY, it shall be referred to two indifferent Persons, one to be chosen by the Assured, the other by the Assurer or Assurers, who shall have full Power to adjust the same; but in Case they cannot agree, then such two Persons shall chuse a Third, and any two of them agreeing, shall be obligatory to both Parties.

It is agreed also between the Assured and Assurers, That in Case of Loss the Money shall not be paid until the Expiration of three Months after Proof is made of the same.

£200.   TWO HUNDRED POUNDS, ... JOHN MIFFLIN.
£100.   ONE HUNDRED POUNDS, ... SAM: M'CALL, JUN'.
£50.   FIFTY POUNDS, ... AUG' HICKS.
£100.   ONE HUNDRED POUNDS for ARCH' M'CALL—SAM: M'CALL, JUN'.

[ENDORSEMENT.]

Policy

Ship *Griffin*,

Joseph Arthur, Mr.

from Philadelphia

to London.

John Kidd.

£450 Goods or Cash,

4 ₱ C'.   Policy, £18.

£185.

Rec'd above Contents,

Jos. Saunders.

Reg'd in Book B, fol. 83,

₱ Jos Saunders.

INDEX.